Decision Tables
in Software
Engineering

Decision Tables in Software Engineering

Richard B. Hurley

IBM Advisory Engineer (Retired)

Van Nostrand Reinhold Data Processing Series

 VAN NOSTRAND REINHOLD COMPANY
NEW YORK   CINCINNATI   TORONTO   LONDON   MELBOURNE

Library of Congress Catalog Card Number: 81-21860
ISBN: 0-442-23599-2

Manufactured in the United States of America

Published by Van Nostrand Reinhold Company Inc.
135 West 50th Street, New York, N.Y. 10020

Van Nostrand Reinhold Publishing
1410 Birchmount Road
Scarborough, Ontario M1P 2E7, Canada

Van Nostrand Reinhold Australia Pty. Ltd.
17 Queen Street
Mitcham, Victoria 3132, Australia

Van Nostrand Reinhold Company Limited
Molly Millars Lane
Wokingham, Berkshire, England

15 14 13 12 11 10 9 8 7 6 5 4 3 2 1

Library of Congress Cataloging in Publication Data
Hurley, Richard B.
    Decision tables in software engineering.

    (Van Nostrand Reinhold data processing series)
    Includes index.
    1. Electronic digital computers–Programming.
2. Decision logic tables. I. Title. II. Series.
QA6.6.H87   001.64'2   81-21860
ISBN 0-442-23599-2   AACR2

Introduction

Some old software tools and techniques mesh well with the new tools and techniques of software engineering. Decision tables are an excellent example. Decision tables preceded software engineering by nearly a decade, but fit so well with software engineering that they might have been created for the purpose.

Four properties of decision tables contribute to the good mesh with software engineering:

1. Decision tables provide a disciplined way to design the interaction of conditions and actions in systems.

2. Decision tables provide automatically, for use in development and maintenance, a concise and standardized documentation of the detailed design of a system.

3. Decision tables provide ways of checking for incompleteness, redundancy, and inconsistency in designs.

4. Decision tables facilitate the transition from design to implementation both in development and maintenance.

Decision Tables in Software Engineering is a how-to book on decision tables, which, as presented here, are widely useful in both system and application software development and maintenance. The focus is on the steps needed to use decision tables in a disciplined manner. Many examples illustrate the steps. The basis for the powerful contribution of decision tables to software development and maintenance is set out here, awaiting your reading.

Ned Chapin
Series Editor

THE VAN NOSTRAND REINHOLD DATA PROCESSING SERIES

Edited by Ned Chapin, Ph.D.

IMS Programming Techniques: A Guide to Using DL/1
  Dan Kapp and Joseph L. Leben

Reducing COBOL complexity Through Structured Programming
  Carma L. McClure

Composite/Structured Design
  Glenford J. Myers

Reliable Software Through Composite Design
  Glenford J. Myers

Top-Down Structured Programming Techniques
  Clement L. McGowen and John R. Kelly

Operating Systems Principles
  Stanley Kurzban, T.S. Heines and A.P. Sayers

Microcomputer Handbook
  Charles J. Sippl

Strategic Planning of Management Information Systems
  Paul Siegel

Flowcharts
  Ned Chapin

Introduction to Artificial Intelligence
    Philip C. Jackson, Jr.

Computers and Management for Business
    Douglas A. Colbert

Operating Systems Survey
    Anthony P. Sayers

Management of Information Technology: Case Studies
    Elizabeth B. Adams

Compiler Techniques
    Bary W. Pollack

Documentation Manual
    J. Van Duyn

Management of ADP Systems
    Marvin M. Wofsey

Hospitals: A System Approach
    Raymon D. Garrett

Hospital Computer Systems and Procedures, Vol I: Accounting Systems
Hospital Computer Systems and Procedures, Vol. I: Accounting Systems
Hospital Computer Systems and Procedures, Vol. II: Medical Systems
    Raymon D. Garrett

Logic Design For Computer Control
    K.N. Dodd

Software Engineering Concepts and Techniques
    John Buxton, Peter Naur and Brian Randell

Information Management Systems: Data Base Primer
    Vivien Prothro

A Programmer's Guide to COBOL
    William J. Harrison

A Guide to Structured COBOL with Efficiency Techniques and
Special Algorithms
    Pacifico A. Lim

Managing Software Development and Maintenance
    Carma L. McClure

Computer-Assisted Data Base Design
    George U. Hubbard

Computer Performance Evaluation: Tools and Techniques for Effective Analysis
    Michael F. Morris and Paul F. Roth

Evaluating Data Base Management Systems
    Judy King

Network Systems
    Roshan Lal Sharma, Ashok D. Inglé and Paulo T. Desousa

Logical Data Base Design
    Robert M. Curtice and Paul E. Jones, Jr.

Decision Tables in Software Engineering
    Richard B. Hurley

CICS/VS Command Level with ANS Cobol Examples
    Pacifico A. Lim

Preface

Decision Tables in Software Engineering is based upon lecture notes I evolved in teaching in industry a course entitled "Decision Table Programming" for programmers and analysts interested in software engineering. The attendees showed an eagerness to learn because they could quickly put the ideas to work in their daily activities.

The approach I have chosen is strictly pragmatic. I attempt to teach the reader what decision tables are, how to formulate them, and how to manipulate them. I do not attempt to develop proofs or to cover theory or to justify why something is done except that it leads to useful results — it works! There is very little mathematical content, and the reader need have no formal mathematical background.

The text is written for practicing programmers, software designers, analysts, testers, documenters, subject-matter specialists, and computer users who have some programming experience.

The material herein evolves, primarily, from five sources:

1. My former engineering background, which consisted heavily of teaching about and designing logic circuits, and making frequent use of the concepts of Boolean algebra (Ref. 13).
2. Both the formal and informal teachings of Frank E. Dapron (9). His class, his written materials, and his many conversations with me have been the real spark behind my teaching and enthusiasm for decision tables.
3. My exposure to software engineering techniques, especially through the counsel of Dr. Ned Chapin, a data processing consultant with InfoSci Inc.

4. My own experience in teaching and using decision tables, before my exposure to Frank Dapron's work. My early convictions were based more on faith than on proven practicalities.
5. The literature, in general, as exemplified in the bibliography. References to that bibliography are placed in parentheses.

When one thinks of programming, one usually thinks of programming languages and lines of coding. However, the principles of decision-table programming require very little in the way of coding and language details. Rather, the concern in the context of software engineering is with a method of problem solving, with a manner of treating a program in small, manageable pieces and tying them together, and with a precise vehicle of communication. Therefore, I stick almost entirely to the *English* language in teaching decision tables — and this book is no exception.

By using English, we also avoid a book that is of only narrow interest. If it were entirely in COBOL, how would the FORTRAN and PL/1 users make out? If we used a smattering of ASSEMBLY, ALGOL, and APL — what would happen to the COBOL, FORTRAN, and PL/1 programmers? In fact, if we increased the number of different languages used, we would either make the book prohibitively large and expensive (assuming we tried to do every problem in all the selected languages), or we would make much of the book unclear to those readers (such as myself) who are not proficient in all the more popular languages (if we treated each problem in a different language).

Decision Tables in Software Engineering is written in the "language of the programmer" — semicode (6), charts (4), functional specifications (8), modules, interrupts, compilers, and so on. However, only on rare occasions do we actually write a line or two of code in a specific *programming source language* — and then we will be in a portion of the book that I consider to be *optional* reading.

Chapter 1 (Background) places decision tables in perspective. It shows where they fit into the scheme of things, it cites a pertinent point in the history of their evolution, and it summarizes most of their applications. Chapter 2 (Introduction) introduces the basic structure of a decision table, and Chapter 3 (Numerics) shows how to calculate a set of numerical values that aid immensely in manipulating tables into desirable forms. Chapter 4 (Furcation) describes the principal methodology for using the numerics of Chapter 3 to prepare a table for implementation.

In Chapter 5 (A Typical Module Development), we carry a problem through all of its stages from "functional specs" to initial table structure to refined tabular form, and finally to a flowchart or semicode implementation. In Chapter 6 (Multimodule Programs), we expand our horizons to handle *complete programs* by several multimodule examples.

Chapter 7 (Some Interesting Tables) treats a variety of tables that illustrate (and show us how to cope with) a number of different, but practical, situations such as incomplete tables, negative logic, and variable-implementation schemes. Chapter 8 (Optimization) introduces the world of decision-table optimization algorithms. However, as stated earlier, we tread with caution here and do not try to penetrate beyond the "point of diminishing returns."

The last three chapters (9, 10, and 11) can be considered optional reading. They represent potentially very useful and important concepts. Yet, a programmer can do an excellent, reliable, efficient, and orderly job of decision-table programming based just on the material in Chapters 1 through 8.

Chapter 9 (Procedural Copying To Produce a DT), shows how to take a given procedurally ordered documentation (an ANSI flowchart, a HIPO diagram, or a Chapin chart) and convert it into a DT — after which, the DT methodology can be employed to ensure completeness, optimize the implementation, compact the documentation, feed a DT processor, and so forth. In turn, this conversion process helps train a programmer to develop a DT so that it will fit with the discipline of structured programming.

As a beautiful example of the practicality of procedural conversion, Frank Dapron took the coding of a very well known and heavily used ASSEMBLY-language subroutine that apparently had been well designed (considering its historical time frame) into 31 statements stored as 31 card images. By converting this coding into DT form and applying some of the procedures described herein, he reduced the coding to 17 lines (storable as 17 card images). This effort created a savings of about 45% of the source code at a cost of about one hour of Frank's time!

Chapter 10 (Boolean Algebra) reverses history somewhat (since the historical foundation of a DT is a logic truth table) by showing how to convert a DT into a set of Boolean algebra functions. Then, it is shown that one has increased freedom (compared to a DT) in manipulating functions to fit certain languages. A very brief review of Boolean algebra is also included. However, the disinterested reader can skip this chapter with little fear of having missed any essential material.

The final chapter, Chapter 11 (Processors), discusses the various methods of automating one or more of the steps between the development of a DT and its ultimate implementation in the machine language of a computer. The various languages employed, and the myriad features to consider if and when selecting a processor, are listed and commented on. However, good DT programming is not dependent on the use of a DT processor — though sometimes significant advantages accrue, especially for subject-matter specialists.

In conclusion, certain incidents have been a most important impetus to the writing of *Decision Tables in Software Engineering*. For example, one day a very competent professional programmer walked into my office, quite worried and confused. He had been attempting for about one month to define a particular module in narrative and flow-diagram form for the software of a particular computer peripheral disk system. So far his efforts had been met with failure — the problem just seemed too complex.

About 45 minutes later he left my office — smiling and amazed. His module definition was complete by means of DT methodology. A couple of days later it was executing successfully on the system.

This office session did not involve any great intelligence or special knowledge of his problem on my part. I only applied a few of the relatively simple concepts presented in the first five chapters of this book.

RICHARD B. HURLEY

Contents

Introduction   v
Preface   xi

1. BACKGROUND   1

    1.1.   Program Design   1
    1.2.   History   2
    1.3.   Applications   4

2. INTRODUCTION   6

    2.1.   Table Structure   6
    2.2.   A Simple Example   8
    2.3.   Table Completeness   10
    2.4.   Exits   16
    2.5.   Don't-Cares   18

3. NUMERICS   23

    3.1.   Initial Composition   23
    3.2.   Mechanical Perfection   24
    3.3.   Some Numerics   29

4. FURCATION   32

    4.1.   Combining Rules   32
    4.2.   More on Completeness   36
    4.3.   Furcation Guide and Sorting   39
    4.4.   Bifurcating the Order Table   40

5. A TYPICAL MODULE DEVELOPMENT   46

    5.1.   Functional Specs   46
    5.2.   Initial Table   47
    5.3.   Row-Sorted Table   52

5.4.   Completely Sorted Table   54
5.5.   Flowchart Implementation   57

6. MULTIMODULE DECISION TABLES   62

6.1.   Functional Specs for Stocks and Bonds   62
6.2.   Modular Structure   65
6.3.   Trade Module   66
6.4.   Accounting   69
6.5.   Bond Table   71
6.6.   Stock Table   73
6.7.   Craps Duel Program   75
6.8.   Craps Duel Modules   77

7. SOME INTERESTING TABLES   85

7.1.   Daily Intake   85
7.2.   Split Personality   87
7.3.   Incomplete Table   90
7.4.   Determining Missing Rules   93
7.5.   Negative Logic   97
7.6.   An Example of Dual Decomposition   100

8. OPTIMIZATION   105

8.1.   Introduction   105
8.2.   Quick and Delayed Rules   106
8.3.   A Pragmatic Pair of Decision Matrix Structuring Rules   111
8.4.   A Sequential Probability Example   113
8.5.   Parallel Testing   115
8.6.   Optimizing Actions   119

9. PROCEDURAL COPYING TO PRODUCE A DT   125

9.1.   Copying a Flowchart   125
9.2.   Copying a HIPO Diagram   127
9.3.   Structured Programming   129
9.4.   Copying a Structured Module   131
9.5.   Which Way to Go   133

10. BOOLEAN ALGEBRA   134

10.1.   Brief Review   134
10.2.   DT Conversion   141

10.3. Implementation   144
10.4. Conclusion   147

11. PROCESSORS   148

11.1. Classification   148
11.2. Languages   149
11.3. Features   150
11.4. Conclusion   154

Bibliography   157
Index   159

Decision Tables
in Software
Engineering

1
Background

1.1. PROGRAM DESIGN

The function-oriented design and implementation practices of software engineering have a weak point: the design of the internal logic of the module or segment. Such internal module designs should be disciplined, easily understood, and checkable. In a top-down environment, those internal designs discipline the entire structure created with the modules.

A module or segment is a formal subdivision of a program or system. It ultimately takes the form of a portion of source code that has a formal beginning (some form of a starting statement) and a formal ending (some form of an ending statement); it is printed contiguously in a listing; and it has a name by which it can be invoked as a unit from anywhere else in the program. Examples include a main PROCEDURE in PL/1, a SECTION in COBOL, a function in APL, a CSECT in S/370 assembly language, and a subroutine in FORTRAN. Hopefully, a module also describes a well-defined, internally cohesive, and externally independent function that works, though such will not be our primary concern herein.

Designing an independent cohesive function is only partially addressed by the function-oriented design techniques of software engineering. It is the thesis of this book that DTs offer an excellent aid in designing the arrangement of functions within a module. This aid is valuable both in the initial design of the modules of the program or system and in the design of the subsequent correcting or enhancing maintenance. The use of DTs fits with a variety of design

1

approaches and documentation aids in software engineering, and tends to compensate for some of their shortcomings (7).

1.2. HISTORY

Written forms (tabular or not), describing combinations of actions and conditions, have been in existence for a time that extends into the indefinite past. That is, written forms have been used that involve questions or tests, sets of potential answers, and the resultant actions to be taken for a given set of answers. A major example of this is the "book" used in such places as a government Social Security office, a police department, a business corporation, a museum, a hospital, a court of law, and so on. In such cases, a member of the organization (who "goes by the book") carries out a prescribed set of actions strictly according to a prescribed set of conditions laid out in the "book." For instance, a manager may make up a set of instructions, based on a (hopefully exhaustive) variety of conditions, that tells a subordinate clerk how to process incoming mail orders or telephone calls, or how to handle potential customers arriving at a display counter in a store or a teller's window in a bank.

In sum, written sets of instructions may be used for person-to-person communication (8). If they are carefully and methodically presented, as in a compact tabular form, they are likely to be less ambiguous and more likely to be easy to interpret than if drawn up in running prose.

Such communication forms may even be made by oneself to oneself. For a very complicated set of daily activities, such as may be the lot of a very busy executive, a rather involved desk calendar may be practically a necessity. Likewise, a person who requires very complex medicinal and dietary restrictions may benefit from a daily guide list of what to eat and drink, and under what circumstances and at what times. A hypothetical self-to-self tabular guide for alternatives in purchasing an automobile is shown in Fig. 1.1.

Tabular forms for computer programs and modules made their appearance in the late 1950s. The General Electric Company (2), the Sutherland Company, and the U.S. Air Force at Norton Air Force Base apparently played a large role in the inauguration of their use (25, 26).

PRICE CAR CONDITION	OVERPRICED	PRICED RIGHT	UNDERPRICED
EXACTLY MEETS ALL DESIRES AND REQUIREMENTS	1. Try to bargain on price. If successful, buy. Else, leave and return next day. 2. Next day, try to bargain on price. Buy regardless.	Try to bargain on price. Buy regardless.	Buy.
NOT PERFECT, BUT SATISFACTORY FOR JOB AT HAND	Reject.	Try to bargain on price. Buy only if successful.	Try to bargain on price. Buy regardless.
NOT ADEQUATE	Reject.	Reject.	Try to bargain at low cost for additional features needed. Buy only if successful.

Fig. 1.1. A simple alternatives table used as a car purchase guide.

More than six person-years had been spent for a complex file-maintenance system in an attempt to define the problem. Flowcharts and narratives had been tried unsuccessfully. Then, in 1958, using decision tables, four analysts needed about four weeks to define the problem successfully.

The Sutherland Company also used tables for problem specification, leaving it up to the programmers to code from the tables. However, the General Electric Company very quickly automated its tables so that a processor could convert the tables directly into source code. The staff at the General Electric Company observed that flowcharts, formulas, and narratives were inadequate when working with complex logic (30).

The concept of using tables for programming first appeared in the literature near the start of the 1960s (see Refs. 1, 11, 15, 23, 29, and 30). The form and names given to the tables also varied a lot. The designation that soon prevailed, of course, was decision tables. That name is often shortened to DT as will often be done herein. Decision tables have even been standardized in Canada (Ref. 10).

Since the decision table was developed before software engineering, the use of a DT is not normally considered a software-engineering technique. Yet the use of decision tables supports well both the theory and practice of software engineering (Refs. 7, 18, 19, 22). Especially noteworthy is that discipline and correctness are automatically emphasized when using DTs.

1.3. APPLICATIONS

While a set of DTs may describe an entire program or system module by module, DTs can do more than just describe software functions. They can be used for at least the following purposes:

1. *To describe a person-to-person task.*   DTs can be used to govern the activities of an individual or a group in carrying out an assignment.
2. *To describe a function to be done by a computer.*   DTs may be used to document the decisions and actions to be done by a computer under the direction of a program.
3. *To define a module in a program or system.*   DTs are a vehicle for "breaking down" or understanding a problem. This use can be painful if the problem is a difficult one. But such a use is quite rewarding and constitutes a "productive disciplined delay" in the chain of events leading to coding and commonly results in a better product.
4. *To aid the parsing work in design.*   DTs can guide the programmer, designer, or analyst in subdividing programs into modules. DTs highlight the interplay of actions and conditions.
5. *To assist in standardizing communication.*   If a group of programmers all use DTs in a disciplined fashion, programs become more readily understandable for all the programmers.
6. *To offer a form of module perfection insurance.*   A methodology exists that can assure that a DT is mechanically perfect. The DT may not direct the reader to do the intended job — the GIGO story (garbage in — garbage out) — but it will direct the reader to do *some* job perfectly.
7. *To serve as a very excellent module-design tool for software engineering.*   Methodologies exist that guide the module designer in organizing the structure of, and even in optimizing certain properties of, a module.
8. *To develop test cases for a module and to help debug it.*   The DT offers a regularized way of exploring the alternative

combinations of possible conditions and of associating actions to be checked with those combinations.

9. *To be input to a DT processor.* To this end, traditional hand-translation of DTs may be dispensed with. The reading of typical source codes (FORTRAN, COBOL, PL/1, APL, ASSEMBLY, and so on) outside of the DT format may even be largely avoided, but only if the programmer uses DTs for both debugging and modification.

2
Introduction

2.1. TABLE STRUCTURE

A DT commonly consists of the four quadrants shown in Fig. 2.1 — *condition stub, action stub, condition entry,* and *action entry,* separated by crossing heavy or double lines. All tests to be specified in the source code for this module are listed in the condition stub — not necessarily in any particular order. All actions to be specified in the code for this module are listed in the action stub, often in a top-to-bottom order according to the sequence in which they are to be executed.

The entry (right-hand) side of the table is vertically subdivided into columns, called *rules*. In the condition-entry quadrant, each rule (column) contains a set of answers to the questions listed in the condition stub, and a set of resultant selected actions to be performed according to a check-off procedure in the action-entry quadrant (horizontally aligned with the particular action statements in the action stub).

A typical decision-table worksheet is pictured in Fig. 2.2. The table header contains the module name. The column numbers identify particular rules. The row numbers near the top of the DT identify the particular conditions (tests or questions) and, below them, the particular actions (functions to be performed). The horizontal double line is added manually to each worksheet at whatever line separates the conditions from the actions in the DT. Of course, a worksheet generally provides space above the illustrated grid structure for such things as module name, program name, page number, programmer name, and date.

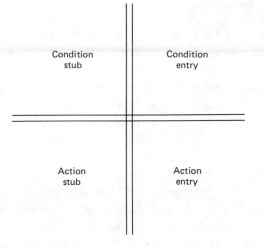

Fig. 2.1. Quadrants of a decision table.

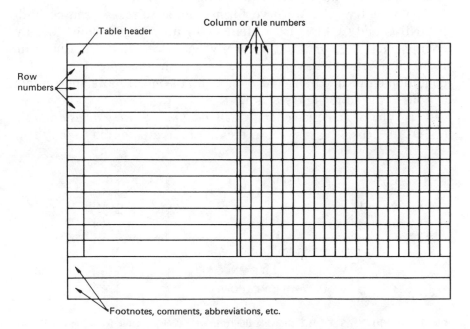

Fig. 2.2. Typical decision-table worksheet for a module.

2.2. A SIMPLE EXAMPLE

Let us suppose we are designing a person-to-person program to guide someone through his activities on a workday. Such a program would likely be composed of many modules — one for each significant activity of the day. We will start this program at the point when he is about to leave the house in the morning and must decide which coat to wear. Obviously this is a trivial problem, but our interest at the moment is simply in the mechanics of a DT and this module's actions that are dependent upon decisions.

Our first attempt may look something like the COAT TABLE of Fig. 2.3. The four quadrants should be evident. There are two conditions, IS IT RAINING? and IS IT COLD?, symbolized as row C1 and C2, respectively, in the condition stub. Note that these conditions are understood to be questions. Hence the "IS IT" and "?" parts are generally omitted. In the action stub, three possible and mutually exclusive actions are indicated: WEAR LINED RAINCOAT, WEAR UNLINED RAINCOAT, or WEAR WOOL OVERCOAT, symbolized by rows A1, A2, and A3, respectively.

On the entry side, we have formed three rules: it can be both RAINING and COLD, just RAINING, or just COLD, symbolized by columns R1, R2, and R3, respectively. Note that for each rule there is a set of answers to the condition-stub questions in the condition-entry quadrant and a selection of one or more appropriate actions in the action-entry quadrant.

This type of table is generally called a *limited entry decision table* (LEDT) because the answers to the questions are limited to only *two*

	COAT TABLE	R1	R2	R3
C1	RAINING	Y	Y	N
C2	COLD	Y	N	Y
A1	WEAR LINED RAINCOAT	X		
A2	WEAR UNLINED RAINCOAT		X	
A3	WEAR WOOL OVERCOAT			X

Fig. 2.3. Initial COAT TABLE showing the form of a decision table for some conditions, actions, and rules.

values, YES (Y) and NO (N), and because the action entries are limited to two possibilities, take the action (X) or do not perform the action (in which case nothing appears). We will illustrate other forms later.

The following table is so simple that it should be readily apparent that there is a missing rule. Should we tabulate all possible sets of answers to our two questions, we get

Y Y N N

Y N Y N

Hence, the all-NO rule is missing. For this rule, R4, we may be tempted to add a fourth action, A4, that says "WEAR NO TOPCOAT." However, this A4 would constitute a redundant action. Physically, it is really not an action at all but the absence of an action. Thus, we simply omit placing an X in any of the A1, A2, or A3 rows instead of adding a meaningless A4. At this point, then, we have already discovered two fairly common DT "pathologies" — *missing rules* and *redundant actions.*

Even with R4 added to our COAT TABLE, this DT would still be incomplete. First, if we had no other actions than the original three, the user would have to spend the rest of the day standing by the coat closet because we have not said where this person should go next. To complete the actions, let us add A4, PROCEED TO GARAGE, to all four of the rules. Thus, we set up the user for the next major activity — selecting a car for the day.

Second, our DT is still inadequate. At the end of each rule we must either include an intermodule connection or end the program. These concluding DT statements are called *exits,* and some DT designers formally include *exit-stub* and *exit-entry* "quadrants" with another set of horizontal double lines to separate the action rows from the exit rows. We will stick to four quadrants, but we will use Xs for module or program exit rows, and, if worksheet space permits, we will leave a blank line between the last action and the first exit. Our position is that a terminating-rule exit *is* a program action, though *not* an internal module action.

In Fig. 2.4, the final COAT TABLE, there is no unique procedure for searching the condition entry for the correct set of answers in a

	COAT TABLE	R1	R2	R3	R4
C1	RAINING	Y	Y	N	N
C2	COLD	Y	N	Y	N
A1	WEAR LINED RAINCOAT	X			
A2	WEAR UNLINED RAINCOAT		X		
A3	WEAR WOOL OVERCOAT			X	
A4	PROCEED TO GARAGE	X	X	X	X
X1	RETURN TO MASTER TABLE	X	X	X	X

Fig. 2.4. Final COAT TABLE.

given execution of the module. We could search the condition entry and stub sequentially, one question at a time, from the top downward or from the bottom upward, or we could search in parallel for the correct, complete set of question answers from left to right or right to left. Second, there is an implication that the actions in any rule are executed sequentially in the action entry and stub from the top downward. For example, in R1, A1 is executed first, A4 second, and X1 third. Third, practical reasons for always searching the condition entry in a DT from top to bottom will be presented later. Fourth, we might have been tempted to state A4 as GO TO GARAGE. However, we are reserving GO TO as a key word to be used only in module exits that would usually be implemented in source code with GO TO. Fifth, the novice may have some difficulty in distinguishing between A4 and X1. Note that in this problem A4 is clearly an action done within the module and done by the user — moving from the clothes closet to the garage. In contrast, X1 tells the user which table to consult for further direction on other matters.

2.3. TABLE COMPLETENESS

For a DT to be complete, each possible, unique combination of question answers or test results must be included exactly once as a rule — no missing rules, no redundant rules, and no contradictory or conflicting rules — and every rule should have a single entrance and a single exit.   Let us suppose that our COAT TABLE contained five rules with the condition-entry pattern:

R1	R2	R3	R4	R5
Y	Y	N	N	Y
Y	N	Y	N	N

If it had, R5 would have been a redundant rule if it contained the same set of actions as R2, both of which characterize a warm rainy day. To correct this, either R2 or R5 should be eliminated. However, if R5 led to a different set of actions than R2, the two rules would be in conflict and we would have a *contradiction.* From such a DT, the user would not know how to behave on a warm rainy day. Either the functional specs (specifications or problem statements) had an error, or the programmer who designed the DT made a mistake. Logic does not supply a resolution between redundant and contradictory rules. Instead, the DT builder must seek guidance from the original specifications.

For an LEDT, the number of distinct elementary rules is

$$2^N$$

where N is the number of conditions. For example, in the four-condition binary tree of Fig. 2.5, note that each condition or test has precisely two possible values or states — YES and NO. Thus, the number of possible rules doubles for each condition. We have already discussed the pattern for two conditions in our COAT table where $N = 2$. Therefore,

$$2^2 = 2 \times 2 = 4$$

and we can identify the four possible combinations in Fig. 2.4 in the four rules R1, R2, R3, and R4.

From Fig. 2.5, it should be clear that for $N = 3$ (using only C1, C2, and C3) we have

$$2^3 = 2 \times 2 \times 2 = 8$$

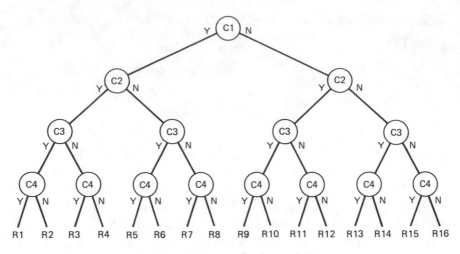

Fig. 2.5. A binary tree for four variables.

combinations. Specifically,

$$
\begin{array}{cccccccc}
Y & Y & Y & Y & N & N & N & N \\
Y & Y & N & N & Y & Y & N & N \\
Y & N & Y & N & Y & N & Y & N \\
\end{array}
$$

For N = 4 we have

$$2^4 = 2 \times 2 \times 2 \times 2 = 16$$

combinations as evidenced by tracing all through every leg of the tree in Fig. 2.5 from R1, yielding the choices YYYY, to R16, yielding the choices NNNN.

Continuing with the workday example, consider the CAR TABLE shown in Fig. 2.6. This time, however, we have changed formats and structured the DT in *extended entry decision table* (EEDT) form. In an EEDT, the stubs do not contain complete questions or actions. Rather, the statements are extended into the entry side of the DT. Also, the condition *moduli* (number of possible values) is no longer necessarily two. Clearly, C1 has a modulus of three (ALONE, WITH FRIEND, and WITH BOSS), and C2 has a modulus of two (GOOD and BAD). Also, an action can take several forms rather than simply

CAR TABLE		R1	R2	R3	R4	R5	R6
C1	EATING LUNCH	ALONE	ALONE	WITH FRIEND	WITH FRIEND	WITH BOSS	WITH BOSS
C2	WEATHER IS	GOOD	BAD	GOOD	BAD	GOOD	BAD
A1	TAKE	OLD CONVERTIBLE	TRUCK	OLD CONVERTIBLE	OLD SEDAN	NEW CONVERTIBLE	NEW SEDAN
A2	DRIVE TO	COMPANY LOT	COMPANY LOT	COMPANY LOT	COMPANY LOT	COMPANY LOT	COMPANY LOT
X1	RETURN TO	MASTER TABLE	MASTER TABLE	MASTER TABLE	MASTER TABLE	MASTER TABLE	MASTER TABLE

Fig. 2.6. CAR TABLE in EEDT format.

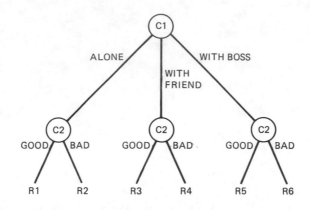

Fig. 2.7. Decision tree for CAR TABLE.

being selected (X) or not selected (nothing appears). Action A1 comes in five varieties — OLD CONVERTIBLE, TRUCK, OLD SEDAN, NEW CONVERTIBLE, and NEW SEDAN, but action A2 and exit X1 are invariant among the various rules.

From either the DT of Fig. 2.6 or the decision tree of Fig. 2.7, it is obvious that there are six elementary rules. There are three possibilities for C1, followed independently by two values for C3, for a product of six combinations. In general, then, the number of *elementary rules* is the *product of the moduli,*

$$\Pi M = M1 \times M2 \times M3 \times \ldots \times MN,$$

where Π represents a product and $M1$ is the modulus of C1, $M2$ of C2, and MN the modulus for the Nth condition. For the CAR TABLE of Fig. 2.6, $N = 2$, $M1 = 3$, and $M2 = 2$, giving us a product of the moduli of

$$M1 \times M2 = 3 \times 2 = 6$$

elementary rules.

In Fig. 2.8 we have our CAR TABLE in a more reasonable format, the *mixed entry decision table* (MEDT). C1 and A1, which are three- and five-valued, respectively, are still presented extended, but C2, A2, and X1 are made limited. Thus, we have three common

CAR TABLE		R1	R2	R3	R4	R5	R6
C1	EATING LUNCH	ALONE	ALONE	WITH FRIEND	WITH FRIEND	WITH BOSS	WITH BOSS
C2	WEATHER GOOD	Y	N	Y	N	Y	N
A1	TAKE	OLD CONVERTIBLE	TRUCK	OLD CONVERTIBLE	OLD SEDAN	NEW CONVERTIBLE	NEW SEDAN
A2	DRIVE TO COMPANY LOT	X	X	X	X	X	X
X1	RETURN TO MASTER TABLE	X	X	X	X	X	X

Fig. 2.8. CAR TABLE in MEDT format.

formats: LEDT, EEDT, and MEDT. The appropriate format depends upon the details of the problem and whether or not (if automated) the source language or the DT processor can accommodate variable and large moduli.

2.4. EXITS

Note that all of the tables so far have had but one exit, RETURN TO MASTER TABLE. Also we have had only one type of exit – namely, RETURN. It is possible for a given table to have several different exits (though only one final exit in each rule) and different kinds of exits.

There are basically five types of exits. One is a *temporary* exit and is listed among the actions. While DO or PERFORM could serve, we will use the key word CALL for this purpose. Its format is

CALL (table name)

When the specified DT [CALL (table name)] has been done, the next marked action in this decision rule is the next action to be taken. Using temporary exits is compatible and common with software engineering.

The other four types of exit, *permanent* exits, are placed in the exit rows. Every rule must end in one of the four permanent exits. They are

RETURN
GO TO (table name)
GO AGAIN
STOP

The outline of a particular DT is sketched symbolically in Fig. 2.9. If the R1 entry pattern happens to represent the results of the condition tests, first F3 (A4) is executed, and then the entire program is terminated, not just the one module, as indicated by the exit STOP, X4.

If R2 applies instead, F1 (A1) is executed; next F2 (A2) is executed; and then a transfer is made to TABLE T2 – GO TO TABLE T2 (X1),

		R1	R2	R3	R4
C1	Q1	Y	Y	N	N
C2	Q2	Y	N	Y	N
A1	F1		X	X	
A2	F2		X		X
A3	CALL TABLE T1			X	
A4	F3	X		X	X
X1	GO TO TABLE T2		X		
X2	GO TO TABLE T3			X	
X3	GO AGAIN				X
X4	STOP	X			

Fig. 2.9. Symbolic skeleton of a particular decision table incompatible with software-engineering techniques.

with no return expected. This is usually associated with a violation of software-engineering techniques. Any DT with any GO TO exit is called an *open* table.

If R3 applies instead, then F1 is executed, followed by a normally temporary exit TABLE T1 – CALL TABLE T1. Any DT entered by means of a CALL should be a *closed* table with RETURN as its permanent exit. Hence, when T1 is performed, the user goes back at the RETURN to the first table containing the CALL, and continues to follow R3 by executing F3 and then exiting to TABLE T3. A DT entered by a temporary exit from another DT is often implemented as a module or subroutine. This is the normal practice when using software-engineering techniques.

Should R4 be activated, F2 is executed, followed by F3, and then the exit taken is GO AGAIN. GO AGAIN causes the *same* DT to be done again. Usually, this is an iteration or looping. To avoid endless loops, any rule that has GO AGAIN as an exit must have at least one marked action that modifies one of the data items explicitly cited in the condition entry for this decision rule. An exception occurs in applications (such as real-time) where the rule asks about the presence or status of an interrupt indicator.

For compatibility with software engineering, GO AGAIN may be used in any number of decision rules when appropriate. But any one

DT should not have both a STOP and a GO TO exit in any rule, let alone the same rule. Thus, the pattern shown in Fig. 2.9 is not compatible with software-engineering techniques because X4 is present in the same DT as X1 or X2.

For compatibility with software engineering, RETURN is the usual permanent exit. The table to return to and the rule and action in that table are usually not specified. Any one DT may be named in more than one CALL. Hence, although the point to return to may vary depending upon the circumstances, it must always be known to, or ascertainable by, the user of the decision table.

Clearly, we have chosen CALL, GO TO, GO AGAIN, STOP, and RETURN as a set of DT keywords or reserved words. Thus, they should only be used as exits. Hence, no condition statement should start with any of these keywords, and no action statement should start with any except CALL [and then only in the CALL (table name) form].

Of course, other keywords could have been chosen, depending on one's preference and the languages or processors are involved. For example, we might have used DO or PERFORM instead of CALL, END instead of STOP, and so on. Also, we could have dispensed with GO AGAIN and simply let a module exit be GO TO (table name) where the table name is the same as the original. However, our set is convenient and adequate, and we will adhere to it herein.

2.5. DON'T-CARES

Let us picture a parlor game called ONE HUNDRED. Each player moves a token along a path of squares on a playing board. There are 125 squares numbered 1 to 125 and colored either red, green, blue, or yellow. A token is moved according to the face-up dot count on a rolled pair of dice and according to the consequences resulting from landing on a square of a certain color (termination of a token move). The object of the game is to be the first player who passes square 100.

Suppose your token is on square 97 and you roll a 6. You thus move your token to square 103, which is red. Landing on a red square means that you lose your next turn. You have passed square 100, however, so you have won the game. Hence, you really don't care whether the square is red since you won't have a next turn. Or suppose you had rolled a 7, moving your token to square 104, which

LANDINGS TABLE	R1
C1 LANDED PAST SQUARE 100	Y
C2 LANDED ON A RED SQUARE	–
•	
•	
•	
A1 POST WINNER	X
A2 SET LOSE-NEXT-TURN SWITCH	
•	
•	
•	

Fig. 2.10. Portion of LANDINGS TABLE in ONE HUNDRED.

is not red. In either case, you have won the game, and the square's color is of no further interest. Therefore, in a DT showing a winning landing, there is no need to test the color. A *don't-care dash* is placed after the square color in the condition entry as shown in an abstract from the LANDINGS TABLE in Fig. 2.10.

The dash in the C2 row of R1 is called a don't-care because, if the game is won, you "don't care" whether the square is red. A dash represents *all* values of the condition test. In an LEDT, a dash represents both a YES and a NO. And in this example, the answer to whether the square was red could have been either YES or NO. Hence, this type of dash is sometimes referred to as an *inclusive* don't-care. Some programmers even use the letter *I* instead of the dash (30). We will generally stick with the dash.

Now let us take a look at Fig. 2.11, a larger abstract from the LAND-INGS TABLE. If your token did not land past square 100, then you *are* concerned with the color of the square and must consider rules R2 to R5. If the square is red (R2), then it could not possibly be green or blue. Thus, there is no need to test for green or blue, and we place don't-care dashes in the C3 and C4 rows of R2.

Mechanically, for the sake of table completeness, don't-care dashes also represent all possible question answers. However, all but one answer, NO in this example, are physically impossible. This

LANDING TABLE	R1	R2	R3	R4	R5
C1 LANDED PAST SQUARE 100	Y	N	N	N	N
C2 LANDED ON A RED SQUARE	–	Y	N	N	N
C3 LANDED ON A GREEN SQUARE	–	–	Y	N	N
C4 LANDED ON A BLUE SQUARE	–	–	–	Y	N
•					
•					
•					
A1 POST WINNER	X				
A2 SET LOSE-NEXT-TURN SWITCH		X			
A3 MOVE TOKEN AHEAD 5 SQUARES			X		
A4 MOVE TOKEN BACK 5 SQUARES				X	
A5 MOVE TOKEN TO SQUARE 50					X
•					
•					
•					

Fig. 2.11. Larger portion of the LANDINGS TABLE.

type of dash is sometimes called a *can't-happen* (13), but more often
an *exclusive* don't-care. Some programmers use an asterisk to represent a condition that can only have a NO answer in a given rule and
a dollar sign for a condition that can only have a YES answer (30).
We will generally use dashes for both types of don't-cares.

Note the color pattern in Fig. 2.11, summarized here:

	R2	R3	R4	R5
RED	Y	N	N	N
GREEN	–	Y	N	N
BLUE	–	–	Y	N

The diagonal of Y's is typical of a set of mutually exclusive conditions. In assembling a set, the normal trick (in order to achieve a
mechanically perfect DT) is to have a diagonal of Y's with N's above
and dashes below, plus a final column of all N's. This final column

LANDINGS TABLE

	R1	R2	R3	R4	R5
C1 LANDED PAST SQUARE 100	Y	N	N	N	N
C2 LANDED ON SQUARE COLORED	–	R	G	B	Y
• • •					
A1 POST WINNER	X				
A2 SET LOSE-NEXT-TURN SWITCH		X			
A3 MOVE TOKEN			AHEAD 5 SQS.	BACK 5 SQS.	TO SQ. 50
• • •					

Fig. 2.12. A MEDT version of LANDINGS TABLE.

represents all other colors, such as YELLOW. Had we made the mistake of having a C5 that tested for YELLOW, we would have introduced another DT pathology — a *redundant condition*. Our all-NO column would represent a square that had some fifth color or no color at all — an impossibility in this problem (though of much merit in an automated process where accidents can happen).

Also note that in R1 (Fig. 2.11), all condition rows in the R1 column below C1 contain a dash, and all rules to the right contain a NO in the C1 row (this would still be true had we shown the complete LANDINGS TABLE DT). Condition C1 is an *overall dominant condition* — a condition so important that it overshadows all other conditions, making it unnecessary to test any other condition. We often refer to such overall dominance as a *fell swooper*.

Incidentally, the LANDINGS TABLE problem is especially suitable for extension, and C2 and A3 are appropriately extended in Fig. 2.12. Note that the dash in row C2 of rule R1 represents all four colors equally, and thus the complex rule R1 includes at least four elementary rules. In fact, if it were not for the high density of dashes in most real DTs, one would be hard pressed to hold a module down to worksheet size or to even be able to work with DTs at all! For example, if, in an LEDT, $N = 10$, the number of elementary rules would be $2^{10} = 1024$; this would hardly fit on a 40-column worksheet or be manageable by a programmer. Yet a module that even approached having 40 complex rules would very likely be unreasonably oversized.

3
Numerics

3.1. INITIAL COMPOSITION

The design of a module or program may be prompted by a narrative statement, by discussions with others involved with the project, by a high-level program sketch (DT, semicode, HIPO package, Chapin chart, and so on), or simply by the programmer's knowing what has to be done and then doing it. For convenience, we will loosely lump all these program design sources into the term *functional specs.*

Consider a module used to guide a clerk as the clerk processes incoming mail orders that have already been screened from other types of incoming mail. The functional specs given to the module designer read as follows (adapted from [13], pp. 8, Situation 4):

1. If the item ordered matches an item we normally stock and the customer is on our approved list, subtract the quantity ordered from our inventory count, assuming we have a sufficient quantity in stock to fill this order. Record all such orders in our transaction log, and see to it that someone ships the merchandise.
2. If the item ordered is not in our inventory list, see to it that someone processes an order rejection.
3. Reject orders from unapproved customers.
4. If the customer's order appears satisfactory, but our inventory is too low, record this order in the follow-up log and see to it that someone takes care of this backorder.

ORDER TABLE		R1	R2	R3	R4	M
C1	ITEM ORDERED IN INVENTORY LIST	Y	N	–	Y	2
C2	CUSTOMER ON APPROVED LIST	Y	–	N	Y	2
C3	SUFFICIENT QUANTITY IN STOCK	Y	–	–	N	2
	CC	1	4	4	1	= 10:8
A1	SUBTRACT QUANTITY ORDERED FROM INVENTORY COUNT	X				
A2	RECORD ORDER IN TRANSACTION LOG	X				
A3	RECORD ORDER IN FOLLOW-UP LOG				X	
A4	CALL SHIP TABLE	X				
A5	CALL REJECT TABLE		X	X		
X1	RETURN	X	X	X	X	

Fig. 3.1. Initial ORDER TABLE.

Our current concern is not whether the functional specs are good or will lead to efficient and reusable modules. Rather, our problem is simply to transfer accurately the functional specs to DT form and to make the DT workable. On our first pass at this tack, we will try to convert the numbered statements to rules.

As we look through the functional specs, we should attempt to identify and sort out all the conditions, actions, and exits. For this problem we will interpret "see to it that someone" to mean a temporary exit to another table that guides another's activities.

In Fig. 3.1 we have listed all the stub items and made an initial attempt at filling in the various rules. Statement 1 led to R1, 2 to R2, 3 to R3, and 4 to R4, and for this simple problem, there should be no difficulty in recognizing these alignments and identifying the appropriate answer lists and action check-offs on the entry side. We have, as best as we can tell, exactly followed the dictates of the various functional-spec statements in formulating each of the various rules.

3.2. MECHANICAL PERFECTION

Note that on the extreme right of the condition-entry quadrant, we have tabulated the condition moduli under the heading M. C1, C2, and

C3 are each of LEDT form, so each has a modulus of 2 (YES or NO). At the bottom of the moduli (M) column is the product of the moduli

$$2 \times 2 \times 2 = 8$$

Hence, our table should contain precisely 8 elementary rules.

Along the bottom of the answer patterns in the condition-entry column is the *column count* (CC) for each of the rules. The column count indicates how many elementary rules are included in a given complex rule. A blank in a test pattern is essentially the equivalent of a dash, representing, at least in initial ignorance, all possible answers. Thus, R2 expands to the pattern

N N N N
Y Y N N
Y N Y N

for a column count of 4. That is, if the item ordered is not in the inventory list, we have an overall dominance or fell swooper. There is apparently no need to test or consider C2 or C3 in deciding to reject the order.

Similarly, R3 expands to the pattern

Y Y N N
N N N N
Y N Y N

of elementary rules, for, again, a column count of 4. Condition C2 is also a fell swooper because if the customer is not on the approved list, we need no further evidence before rejecting the order.

Thus, R2 and R3 appear to be good rules. However, we note that they caused the total CC to be 10, but the moduli product is only 8, as shown in the 10:8 comparison in Fig. 3.1. Rules R2 and R3 clearly overlap, for each, in expansion, contains the same two patterns

N N
N N
Y N

Thus, R2, in its fell swooping, includes all rules with the first row C1 = N; R3, in its fell swooping, includes all rules in which the second row C2 = N. Fortunately, however, R2 and R3 lead to the same action set (namely, X2), so we have a curable rule redundancy rather than an incurable conflict or contradiction.

Patterns for a set of independent fell swoopers can be resolved in much the same way as patterns for mutually exclusive conditions. For a *positive* example of 3 fell swoopers, the pattern can be resolved as

$$
\begin{array}{cccc}
Y & N & N & N \\
- & Y & N & N \\
- & - & Y & N
\end{array}
$$

by placing dashes below the Ys and Ns above the Ys, plus a final all-NO column. For a *negative* example of 3 fell swoopers (and likewise for 3 exclusives), the pattern can be resolved as

$$
\begin{array}{cccc}
N & Y & Y & Y \\
- & N & Y & Y \\
- & - & N & Y
\end{array}
$$

by placing dashes below the Ns and Ys above the Ns, with a final all-YES column. The N diagonal fits our C1-C2 fell swoopers, so we could place a Y in the first row of R3 for the pattern

	R2	R3	R4
C1	N	Y	Y
C2	-	N	Y

Now R3 no longer contains the troublesome

$$
\begin{array}{cc}
N & N \\
N & N \\
Y & N
\end{array}
$$

pattern, removing the overlap between R2 and R3 and reducing the R3 CC to 2.

	R1	R2	R3	R4	M
C1	Y	N	Y	Y	2
C2	Y	–	N	Y	2
C3	Y	–	–	N	2
CC	1	4	2	1	= 8:8
A1	X				
A2	X				
A3				X	
A4	X				
A5		X	X		
X1	X	X	X	X	

Fig. 3.2. Symbolic skeleton of ORDER TABLE in a mechanically perfect version.

Alternatively, we could have placed the dashes above the diagonal and the *explicit* or *salient values* (that is, Ys or Ns) below, if we had so chosen.

For a DT to be mechanically perfect, it must meet three conditions:

1. Every rule must end in a permanent exit.
2. The summation of the column count must equal the product of the moduli:

$$\Sigma CC = \Pi M$$

3. The condition entries for each and every rule must be unique.

Clearly, in Fig. 3.2, incorporating our fell-swooper diagonal "fix," we have achieved the first two rules for mechanical perfection. Only the uniqueness requirement remains to be established.

Consider the LEDT pattern

	R1	R2	R3	R4	
	Y	N	Y	Y	
	Y	–	N	Y	
	Y	–	–	Y	
CC	1	4	2	1	= 8

This would have had the correct CC, but rules R1 and R4 have the same answer set. Thus, we would have either a contradiction or a redundancy between R1 and R4. Also consider the pattern

	R1	R2	R3	R4		
	Y	N	N	Y		
	Y	–	N	Y		
	Y	–	–	N		
CC	1	4	2	1	=	8

Again we have the correct CC (for 3 LEDT conditions), but rules R2 and R3 overlap. That is, R2 includes R3, and there will be either a conflict or a redundancy. R2 expands as

$$N \quad N \quad N \quad N$$
$$Y \quad Y \quad N \quad N$$
$$Y \quad N \quad Y \quad N$$

and R3 expands as

$$N \quad N$$
$$N \quad N$$
$$Y \quad N$$

matching the last two elementary rules in R2. Hence, it is not sufficient for the sum of the column count to simply match the product of the moduli.

   To ensure uniqueness, every rule must take a different path or set of paths along the decision tree, as occurs in the binary tree of Fig. 2.5. A methodical procedure for checking uniqueness is presented in the Fig. 3.2 version of the ORDER TABLE. Rule R1 is compared with each of the other rules. If unique, then R2 is compared with each of the remaining rules. Finally, R3 is compared with R4. In each of these comparisons, we are looking for at least one row in which the answers are clearly different. We deal only with salient or explicit values, ignoring dashes since a dash can never be different than anything in that row.

In Fig. 3.2, the C1 Y in R1 is different than the C1 N in R2. Thus, R1 and R2 are different. Next, the C2 Y in R1 is different than the C2 N in R3. Hence, R1 is different than R3. Finally, the C3 Y in R1 is different than the C3 N in R4. Therefore, we have established that rule R1 is unique since it differs from all other rules.

Working with the reduced set of R2, R3, and R4, we note that the C1 N in R2 is different than the C1 Y in both R3 and R4. Hence, R2 is unique. Finally, R3 and R4 differ in the C2 row. So all four rules are unique and Fig. 3.2 does, indeed, represent a mechanically perfect table.

The proof of mechanical perfection goes a long way in assuring a programmer that he or she has a good DT. It gives the programmer some relatively low-cost insurance, even if DTs are not being used for any other purpose such as module design or documentation.

3.3. SOME NUMERICS

The decision portion of the mechanically perfect version of the OR-DER TABLE has been reproduced in Fig. 3.3 along with some calculated values we will simply call *numerics*. Two of these numerics we have already treated — the column count (CC) and the condition moduli (M).

The next set of numerics is called the *row count matrix* (RCM). It contains a simple tabulation of each of the explicit values and a dash count. The counts should be apparent. In row C1 there are exactly 3 rules with a Y, 1 with an N, and none with a dash. In row C2 there are 2 rules with Ys, 1 with an N, and 1 with a dash. And in row C3 there is 1 rule with a Y, 1 with an N, and 2 with dashes. If an RCM column is for an impossible entry for the condition, a blank,

	R1	R2	R3	R4	M	RCM Y	N	–	WDC	DEL	DOM
C1	Y	N	Y	Y	2	3	1	0	0	2	C2, C3
C2	Y	–	N	Y	2	2	1	1	4	1	C3
C3	Y	–	–	N	2	1	1	2	6	0	
CC	1	4	2	1 = 8:8							

Fig. 3.3. Symbolic decision half of ORDER TABLE with some added numerics.

not a zero, is put in the RCM. We need not be concerned, yet, with what these numerics are used for — simply with how to determine them.

Note that the last column in the RCM is a *dash-count* (DC) tabulation. The following column is a *weighted dash count* (WDC) listing. A WDC is based on the dash count. As a dash is added to the count, it is weighted by the column count of the rule in which it is found. Thus, for row C2, the dash in R2 is given a weight of 4 since that is the only dash in row C2; its WDC = 4 (1 X 4 = 4) since the CC is 4. In the C3 row, there are 2 dashes. The first is weighted by CC = 4 from R2, and the second is weighted by CC = 2 from R3, for a total WDC = 6: (1 X 4) + (1 X 2) = 6. Of course, there are no dashes in row C1, so its WDC = 0.

The next column is called DEL, for Greek delta, a symbol used here to represent a difference. For an LEDT, the DELs are simply the unsigned numerical differences between the Y and N (nondash) counts in the RCM of each row. For the C1 row, 3 – 1 = 2. For the C2 row, 2 – 1 = 1. And for the C3 row, 1 – 1 = 0. Dashes are always ignored when computing DELs.

Suppose we have an EEDT with an RCM as follows:

	A	B	C	D	–
C1	3	2	2	2	1
C2	0	5	4	1	0
C3	0	1	3	3	3
C4	1	1	6	2	0

That is, each of the four conditions has a modulus of 4 (four different answers symbolized as *A, B, C,* and *D*). In the general case, the DEL is the absolute (ABS) value of the largest explicit value minus the sum of all the other explicit values. Thus, for row C1, the DEL is

$$\text{ABS}\{3-(2+2+2)\} = \text{ABS}\{3-6\} = \text{ABS}\{-3\} = 3$$

For row C2,

$$\text{ABS}\{5-(4+1)\} = \text{ABS}\{5-5\} = \text{ABS}\{0\} = 0$$

For row C3,

$$\text{ABS}\{3-(1+3)\} = \text{ABS}\{3-4\} = \text{ABS}\{-1\} = 1$$

And for row C4,

$$\text{ABS}\{6-(1+1+2)\} = \text{ABS}\{6-4\} = \text{ABS}\{2\} = 2$$

The final numeric in Fig. 3.3 is a *dominance* (DOM) listing. It tells us which conditions tend to dominate others, possibly allowing us to eliminate testing on those that are dominated — an overall fell swooper is a grand example of a condition that tends to dominate *all* other conditions. Mechanically, DOMs can be detected in a table by exercising the guide:

A given condition row dominates another condition row if for all rules which have dashes in the other condition row, the given condition row has no dashes where the degree of dominance is measured by a count of the number of qualifying dashes in the other condition row.

For a DT sorted for all but dominance (see Section 4.3), an alternative guide is:

A condition row containing one or more dashes is dominated by all the condition rows above it in which the rules from above the nondashes entries in this condition row are uniquely different from each of the rules containing the dashes in this row.

Let us apply the first guide to in Fig. 3.3. C1 contains 3 Ys. However, no other row contains three dashes vertically aligned with these 3 Ys. On the other hand, C1 contains only 1 N that is vertically aligned with a dash in both the C2 and the C3 rows. Therefore, all the Ns in C1 align with dashes in C2 and C3, so C1 dominates both C2 and C3. Similarly, the one and only N in C2 is vertically aligned with a dash in C3, so C2 dominates C3.

Dominance is only a concern to the DT builder or user if the DT is to be implemented by the use of a sequential testing procedure (34). A dash represents an indifference to the results of a test, or, alternatively, that a test is not relevant or may be omitted or skipped. A nondash specifies a position on a test. Hence, these nondash tests must take precedence and are controlling. With few tests to make, the dominance is obvious among the tests. When many conditions are present, the patterns become complex and not obvious. The dominance guides unravel the complexity when testing is to be used in implementing decision tables.

4
Furcation

4.1. COMBINING RULES

Rules often can (and generally should) be combined if they have identical action (action-exit) sequences. In particular, if we have an LEDT, then rules with identical actions can be combined exactly two at a time if their condition patterns are exactly the same except for one explicit value. That is, the two rules must be identical in *all* respects except that they have clearly opposite values for precisely one condition.

Consider the two rules

	R1	R2
C1	Y	Y
C2	N	Y
C3	–	–
C4	N	N
A1	X	X
A2		
X1	X	X

Note that R1 and R2 have the same action-entry checkoffs and differ only in their answers to C2. Thus, it makes no difference whether C2 is YES or NO. In either case, the answers to the other conditions are the same and the actions are the same. Thus, C2 is really an inclusive don't-care, and these two CC = 2 rules can be combined into the one CC = 4 rule:

	R1/R2
C1	Y
C2	–
C3	–
C4	N
A1	X
A2	
X1	X

In this example we have uncovered a general but partial guide governing all combinable rules — they must have equal column counts. An exception for EEDT occurs when combining rules having opposite or negative values. An example is combining two rules having = and < entries on a row, but having the same CC. After combining, the resulting ≤ rule has twice the CC of either of the original rules. Yet that resulting rule can be combined with a candidate rule having a > entry for the row (since <, =, and > are the only possibilities), resulting in a dash rule.

Let's look at a portion of another LEDT where all the rules abstracted, and only these rules, have the same action set. Since we are only working with the condition numbers and rules numbers, we will simplify our column and row numbers by omitting the Cs and the Rs:

	1	2	3	4	5	6	7	8
1	Y	Y	Y	Y	Y	Y	Y	Y
2	N	N	Y	Y	Y	N	N	Y
3	Y	N	Y	N	Y	N	Y	N
4	N	N	Y	N	N	Y	Y	Y
CC	1	1	1	1	1	1	1	1

Because all these rules have the same set of action selections and the same CC, they are all candidates for combining pairwise. Working left to right, note that rules 1 and 2 differ explicitly only in row 3. Also, rules 3 and 5 differ only in row 4. Rules 4 and 8 differ only in row 4, and, finally, rules 6 and 7 are identical but for row 3. Making these four combinations, we get

	1/2	3/5	4/8	6/7
1	Y	Y	Y	Y
2	N	Y	Y	N
3	–	Y	N	–
4	N	–	–	Y
CC	2	2	2	2

Again we have rules with identical CCs, so they may be combinable. Rules 1/2 and 6/7 differ only in row 4, and rules 3/5 and 4/8 have opposite values in row 3. Making these further combinations, we now have

	1/2/6/7	3/5/4/8
1	Y	Y
2	N	Y
3	–	–
4	–	–
CC	4	4

Again we observe equal CCs, and here we have a different test result only for condition 2. So, finally, we have achieved an extreme case of combinability:

	1/2/6/7/3/5/4/8
1	Y
2	–
3	–
4	–
CC	8

We recognize a fell swooper. Namely, C1 apparently is an overall dominant condition in the four-condition table we abstracted from.

When we have extended conditions in a DT and encounter a moduli other than two, combinability is slightly more demanding. We still must have identical action sets, and we still must have rules with equal column counts differing in only one salient condition value. However, if the one condition value that is explicitly different has a modulus of three, for instance, then we must combine rules precisely three at a time. In general, whatever the modulus of the differing condition is, the modulus tells us how many rules must be combined at one time.

Let us look at an abstracted portion of an MEDT having four conditions and a moduli product of 48. We are concerned, at the moment, with only a quarter of this table (one-fourth of the elementary rules). Let us assume that these rules, and only these rules, all lead to the same action set and their condition patterns are

	1	2	3	4	5	6	M
1	Y	Y	Y	Y	Y	Y	2
2	–	1	2	–	4	3	4
3	N	N	N	N	N	N	2
4	A	B	B	C	B	B	3
CC	4	1	1	4	1	1	48

Note that rules 1 and 4 each have a CC = 4 because their single dash in row 2 represents a modulus 4 condition that can assume the values 1, 2, 3, or 4. Thus, a C2 dash represents four different elementary rules. Rules 1 and 4 are candidates for combination. They differ in row 4 where rule 1 has an A and rule 4 holds a C. But row 4 has a modulus of 3, so such rules must be combined 3 at a time — we need another rule, identical to rules 1 and 4, but that shows a B in the C4 row.

Moving on to rule 2, we note that rules 2, 3, 5, and 6 match except for row 2. Since row 2 is modulus 4, and we have four rules each with a different explicit value, these four rules are combinable. Our MEDT option now looks like

	1	2/3/5/6	4
1	Y	Y	Y
2	–	–	–
3	N	N	N
4	A	B	C
CC	4	4	4

These three rules are now also combinable since they differ only in row 4, which has a modulus of three, yielding

	1/2/3/5/6/4	M
1	Y	2
2	–	4
3	N	2
4	–	3
CC	12	48

As an aid in calculating the CC for the conditions of a rule, start from the top and multiply going downward. Wherever there is an explicit value, multiply by one, and wherever there is a dash, multiply by the modulus of that row. Thus, for the final rule above, the column count is

$$CC = 1 \times 4 \times 1 \times 3 = 12$$

4.2. MORE ON COMPLETENESS

For a DT to be mechanically perfect, every rule must end in a permanent exit and the condition pattern must be complete (as discussed in Section 3.2). Completeness requires that, simultaneously,

1. $\Sigma CC = \Pi M$.
2.   Each condition pattern must be unique.

We will normally employ a left-to-right check-off scheme (as we did in the prior chapter) to prove the uniqueness of each rule separately. However, we should be aware that there are two other methods that check for both of the stated completeness requirements.

One method is the *classical technique* (21). A classical expansion or matrix of all possible elementary rules is drawn up, and then the DT in question is either composed by successively combining rules (that can be combined); or the classical expansion is used as a check-off matrix for the DT already composed. We shall examine the check-off of a given DT by comparing it with a complete decision matrix of elementary rules.

A classical expansion of an LEDT three-decision matrix is

	1	2	3	4	5	6	7	8
C1	Y	Y	Y	Y	N	N	N	N
C2	Y	Y	N	N	Y	Y	N	N
C3	Y	N	Y	N	Y	N	Y	N

The last version of our ORDER TABLE (Fig. 3.3) is reproduced in Fig. 4.1. Observe that R1 checks off (matches or accounts for column 1 in the above elementary matrix. In Fig. 4.1, R2 includes columns 5, 6, 7, and 8 (all rules with a C1 of N) of the classical expansion. R3 covers columns 3 and 4 (all rules starting with C1 = Y and C2 = N), and R4 matches column 2. Since the DT in Fig. 4.1 exactly accounts for each and every rule exactly once in the classical expansion, we have simultaneously proved that we have both a correct total CC and that each of the rules is unique.

Unless automated, the classical proof technique is impossibly time-consuming and laborious for more than a few conditions. For example, recall that an LEDT having $N = 10$ conditions would require 1024 patterns (of 10 values each)!

Another method takes the condition entries of a given table, ignores all actions, and successively combines various condition

	R1	R2	R3	R4	M	RMC Y	RMC N	RMC –	WDC	DEL	DOM
C1	Y	N	Y	Y	2	3	1	0	0	2	C2, C3
C2	Y	–	Y	N	2	2	1	1	4	1	C3
C3	Y	–	–	N	2	1	1	2	6	0	
CC	1	4	2	1 = 8:8							

Fig. 4.1. Symbolic decision half of ORDER TABLE with some added numerics.

patterns.   If the final result is precisely one single pattern of all
dashes, then it can be assumed that no rules were missing and there
were no extraneous (redundant or conflicting) rules.

Using the decision matrix from Fig. 4.1, we have

	R1	R2	R3	R4
C1	Y	N	Y	Y
C2	Y	–	N	Y
C3	Y	–	–	N
CC	1	4	2	1

Ignoring actions, R1 and R4 combine to yield

	R1/R4	R2	R3
C1	Y	N	Y
C2	Y	–	N
C3	–	–	–
CC	2	4	2

Next, R1/R4 combines with R3 for

	R1/R4/R3	R2
C1	Y	N
C2	–	–
C3	–	–
CC	4	4

And finally, these two rules combine to give

R1/R4/R3/R2

C1	−
C2	−
C3	−
CC	8

and we have proved, once again, that our ORDER TABLE has a perfectly complete set of decision patterns.

It appears that for pencil-and-paper DT development, the check-off procedure introduced in the prior chapter is most convenient and flexible as a table grows and is refined. However, the second method affords us a speedy and excellent confirmation for a completed DT. Moreover, being a different method, it provides some insurance (perhaps akin to parity checking) that we did not make an error by the earlier technique.

4.3. FURCATION GUIDE AND SORTING

For the most part herein, we will use semicode (6), flow diagrams, or Chapin charts (4, 6) to implement our DTs, rather than use source codes in arbitrarily chosen languages or inputs to arbitrarily selected DT processors. This gimmick should permit us to learn DT development in a clear and easily understandable manner. However, our approach should not be construed as an endorsement of any particular tool for any other purpose than as used here − as a means to illustrate a process.

Parsing and *furcation* are terms used by people who work with DTs to indicate the hopefully efficient breaking up or decomposition of a DT into orderly smaller pieces, usually to make the DT more readily understandable or workable (5). In particular, for an LEDT, decomposition is called *bi*furcation. If every condition were modulus three, the particular term would be *tri*furcation, and that is about where the English language leaves off. The general term, of course, is simply furcation.

A set of steps that has served well as a guide to the furcation or parsing of DTs is as follows:

1. Develop a mechanically perfect DT.
2. Combine all rules that can be combined.
3. Ensure that at least one condition row contains no dashes — expand a minimum dash row if necessary.
4. Calculate the RCM (row count matrix), the WDC (weighted dash count), and the DEL (delta or difference) numerics.
5. *Row sort* the conditions, from the top row downward, in ascending WDCs (this is the major sort).
6. Sort separately the sets of rows with equal WDCs, from the top row downward, in ascending DELs (this is the intermediate sort).
7. Calculate the DOM (dominance) numerics.
8. Sort rows separately by placing dominant rows above the rows they dominate for any conflicting dominances (this is the minor sort). Skip this step if, for example, row 4 dominated row 6 but row 6 also dominated row 4.
9. *Column sort* the rules, working from the top row downward, row by row, in a reasonable left-to-right sequence such as Y before N before — in an LEDT, A before B before C before —, and 1 before 2 before 3 before — in an MEDT or EEDT.
10. Finally, for convenience of reference, renumber all the conditions and rules for orderly top-to-bottom and left-to-right sequencing, respectively.

4.4. BIFURCATING THE ORDER TABLE

The ORDER TABLE in Fig. 4.1 has already been checked for mechanical perfection (step 1 in our furcation guide). Referring back to Fig. 3.2, the only rules with identical action sets are R2 and R3. Since these two rules have different CCs, no rules may be combined (step 2). We already have one row (C1) with no dashes (step 3), and we have already calculated the RCM, WDC, and DEL columns (step 4) in Fig. 4.1.

The conditions have been sorted in ascending WDC order from the top (step 5), and since no conditions have equal WDCs, no DEL subsorting (step 6) is necessary. Moreover, the DOMs (step 7) already have the dominant rows above those they dominate (step 8). Therefore, we already have a DT in good shape and fully row sorted.

To column sort (step 9), we first row sort on the conditions in the first row, C1, placing the Ys ahead of the Ns.

				2
1	Y	Y	Y	N
2				–
3				–

Note that in the process of column sorting row 1, we just happened to uniquely identify rule 2 (since it was the only rule starting with N), so we filled it in vertically.

Now in column sorting row C2, we maintain a Y before N before – sequence under the Ys of row 1.

			3	2
1	Y	Y	Y	N
2	Y	Y	N	–
3			–	–

In the process of column sorting row 2, we uniquely identified (and filled in) rule 3. Finally, sticking to our chosen left-to-right sequencing, we column sort row 3, placing a Y first and an N second, under the Ys in row 2.

	1	4	3	2
1	Y	Y	Y	N
2	Y	Y	N	–
3	Y	N	–	–

	R1	R2	R3	R4
C1	Y	Y	Y	N
C2	Y	Y	N	–
C3	Y	N	–	–
A1	X			
A2	X			
A3		X		
A4	X			
A5			X	X
X1	X	X	X	X

Fig. 4.2. Symbolic skeleton of ORDER TABLE after the ten furcation guide steps.

The finalized ORDER TABLE, after renumbering the rules (step 10), is pictured in Fig. 4.2. The DT matrix, renumbered, now appears as

	1	2	3	4
1	Y	Y	Y	N
2	Y	Y	N	–
3	Y	N	–	–

Observe how readily it can be bifurcated to the point of making its implementation obvious:

C1	Y	Y	Y	N
C2	Y	Y	N	–
C3	Y	N	–	–
	R1	R2	R3	R4
	Actions	Actions	Actions	Actions

as illustrated by Fig. 4.3.

In implementing DTs in a source code, the execution time and the storage space needed may be of concern if alternate implementations in source code are being evaluated. Thus, we might count the predicates (tests) for a given furcation. In Fig. 4.3, this count is clearly 3 — each of three conditions is stored for testing precisely once.

Other programming rules employ guide steps that are intended to minimize the average execution time of decisions. Assuming, as either a point of standardization or a state of ignorance, that all rules are equally likely to occur in a given DT execution, we might also observe this "figure of merit" for our DT. In Fig. 4.3 (or

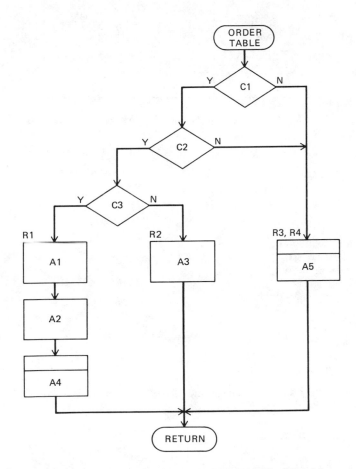

Fig. 4.3(a). Flow diagram for the ORDER TABLE of Fig. 4.2.

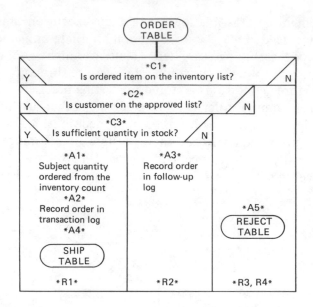

Fig. 4.3(b). Chapin chart for the ORDER TABLE of Fig. 4.2 (4,6).

ORDER TABLE

INPUT

Transaction log
Follow-up log
Inventory list
Ordered item identification
Approved customer list
Customer identification
Quantity ordered
Inventory count or quantity in stock

OUTPUT

Transaction log
Follow-up log
Inventory count

Fig. 4.3(c). Semicode for the ORDER TABLE of Fig. 4.2 (6).

FUNCTIONS

START PROCESS ORDER TABLE

IF ordered item is on inventory list NOTE: C1
    IF customer is on approved list NOTE: C2
        IF sufficient quantity is in stock NOTE: C3
            Subtract quantity ordered from inventory count NOTE: A1, R1
            Record order in transaction log NOTE: A2
            Perform SHIP TABLE NOTE: A4
        ELSE not enough quantity is in stock NOTE: C3
            Record order in follow-up log NOTE: A3, R2
        END-IF
    ELSE customer is not on approved list NOTE: C2
        Perform REJECT TABLE NOTE: A5, R3
    END-IF
ELSE ordered item is not on approved list NOTE: C1
    Perform REJECT TABLE NOTE: A5, R4
END-IF
END PROCESS ORDER TABLE

Fig. 4.3(c.) Continued

directly from the DT of Fig. 4.2), it is clear that it takes the execution of 3 tests (C1 = Y, C2 = Y, and C3 = Y) to reach the action set of R1 (A1, A2, and X1), 3 tests to reach the action set of R2, 2 tests for R3, and but one test (C1 = N) for R4. Hence, the average number of tests per execution (assuming a 25% probability for each of our 4 rules) is

$$(3 + 3 + 2 + 1) \div 4 = 9/4 = 2.25$$

5
A Typical Module Development

5.1. FUNCTIONAL SPECS

Let us apply what we have already discussed to build a DT for a single module. We shall call this modest one-module decision table LIQUID INVESTMENT. A narrative description follows:

You have decided to try to beat the rising prices of white wines by stocking up for a year. You have just entered your favorite neighborhood wine store — a large place with an extensive offering in the California-wine section. You are attempting, at minimum cost, to stock up now on varietal California white wines (such as Chenin Blanc, Emerald Riesling, Semillon, and so on) from Monterey county, Napa county, and Sonoma county.

You are only interested in the 1.5-liter sizes, and you want to buy two or three containers of each wine selected. Also, you are limiting yourself to wines that are currently selling at a special discount sale price and are under $7 per bottle or whose regular price is below $6. Moreover, you will only buy in full-case amounts (6 containers — can be mixed wines) in order to get the 10% case discount.

The DT should guide your wine selection activities through the California-wine section, and include passing through the checkout line, paying for the wines selected, and leaving the wine store.

We will assume that all California white wines are located in one contiguous section, that our search will follow the sequence of wine displayed in that section, and that all candidates selected are placed in the checkout cart individually as they are discovered.

5.2. INITIAL TABLE

As we scan through the functional specs, let us make a list of tests, as follows:

C1. Is it a California white varietal wine?
C2. Is the origin Monterey, Napa, or Sonoma?
C3. Is it in a 1.5-liter container?
C4. Is it selling at a special sale price?
C5. Is its price under $7?
C6. Is its price under $6?
C7. Have we passed the end of the California-wine section?

In the same way, let us make a list of actions:

A1. Put selected containers of wine in the cart.
A2. Advance to next California wine displayed.
A3. Return (at end of search) any excess containers that will not fill a case of 6.
A4. Pass through the checkout and pay for wine selected.
A5. Leave the store.

The only exits appear to be:

X1. GO AGAIN (to examine next wine displayed).
X2. STOP (if we have completed our pass through the California-wine section, checked out, and left the store).

We could try to do a little mental presorting (and eventually we will learn the tricks here), but at this point a brute-force solution will give us more practice at sorting (and begin to reveal some of the tricks).

A typical first pass in composing our table is illustrated in Fig. 5.1. Let us study it rule by rule. In rule R1, we have a candidate that meets all our requirements. Since it is on special sale and below $7, we need not test for it possibly being also under $6. In R2, we have a candidate not offered at a special discount, so we only test for its regular price being under $6. In either rule, we put one or two containers in the cart, proceed to (*not* GO TO) the next display section,

LIQUID INVESTMENT		1	2	3	4	5	6	7	8	M
C1	CALIFORNIA WHITE VARIETAL	Y	Y	Y	N	Y	Y	Y	–	2
C2	3-COUNTY ORIGIN	Y	Y	Y	–	N	Y	Y	–	2
C3	1.5-LITER SIZE	Y	Y	Y	–	–	N	Y	–	2
C4	SPECIAL DISCOUNT SALE	Y	N	N	–	–	–	–	–	2
C5	PRICE BELOW $7	Y	–	–	–	–	–	–	–	2
C6	PRICE BELOW $6	–	Y	N	–	–	–	–	–	2
C7	PASSED END OF CALIFORNIA WINE SECTION	N	N	N	N	N	N	N	Y	2
	CC	2	2	2	32	16	8	8	64 = 134:128	
A1	PUT CONTAINER IN CART	X	X							
A2	PROCEED TO NEXT WINE	X	X	X	X	X	X	X		
A3	RETURN EXCESS CONTAINERS								X	
A4	CHECK OUT AND PAY								X	
A5	LEAVE THE STORE								X	
X1	GO AGAIN	X	X	X	X	X	X	X		
X2	STOP								X	

Fig. 5.1. First pass on LIQUID INVESTMENT.

and then run the new wine all through our table (GO AGAIN). In R3, the price is too high, so we simply go on to the next wine displayed.

Now, starting with R4, we set up a "second-level" fell swooper pattern. We recognize that California white varietal wine, origin in Monterey, Napa, or Sonoma, and 1.5-liter size are each equally dominant conditions. So in R4, R5, and R6 we have a negative fell-swooper diagonal of Ns and R4, R5, and R6, followed by an all-YES column in R7.

We called C1, C2, and C3 second-level fell swoopers because the most dominant condition of all is C7, "passed end of California-wine section." It is the one and only true or "first-level" overall fell swooper as evidenced by all the don't-cares in R8. Its actions, of course, are the terminating ones of returning excess containers, making out the check, and leaving the store. We then conclude (STOP).

A check of the total CC and the moduli product shows we have too many rules. Next we recognize that our R7 all-YES rule includes, and conflicts with, rules R1, R2, and R3, which also have all Ys in the first three rows.

A classical expansion of R7 gives us

	a	b	c	d	e	f	g	h
1	Y	Y	Y	Y	Y	Y	Y	Y
2	Y	Y	Y	Y	Y	Y	Y	Y
3	Y	Y	Y	Y	Y	Y	Y	Y
4	Y	Y	Y	Y	N	N	N	N
5	Y	Y	N	N	Y	Y	N	N
6	Y	N	Y	N	Y	N	Y	N
7	N	N	N	N	N	N	N	N

Expanding R1, R2, and R3 yields

	R1		R2		R3	
1	Y	Y	Y	Y	Y	Y
2	Y	Y	Y	Y	Y	Y
3	Y	Y	Y	Y	Y	Y
4	Y	Y	N	N	N	N
5	Y	Y	Y	N	Y	N
6	Y	N	Y	Y	N	N
7	N	N	N	N	N	N

Comparing the two expansions, it is clear that R1 matches columns *a* and *b* in the R7 expansion, R2 matches columns *e* and *g* in R7, and R3 matches *f* and *h*. Furthermore, R1 and R2 yield candidate wines whereas R7 does not. Hence, we have made a mistake, so we reduce R7 to only the remaining expansion columns *c* and *d*. These two patterns clearly account for an otherwise acceptable wine that is still too expensive (not below $7) even though it *is* on special sale.

A symbolic version of our corrected table appears in Fig. 5.2. Every rule ends in an exit and the total CC matches the moduli product. Therefore, we need only prove rule uniqueness to guarantee a mechanically perfect module. Since uniqueness proofs are generally somewhat confusing at first, we will go through this table very systematically, working left to right and top to bottom. (Recall that

	R1	R2	R3	R4	R5	R6	R7	R8	M	RCM Y	N	–	WDC	DEL
C1	Y	Y	Y	N	Y	Y	Y	–	2	6	1	1	64	5
C2	Y	Y	Y	–	N	Y	Y	–	2	5	1	2	96	4
C3	Y	Y	Y	–	–	N	Y	–	2	4	1	3	112	3
C4	Y	N	N	–	–	–	Y	–	2	2	2	4	120	0
C5	Y	–	–	–	–	–	N	–	2	1	1	6	124	0
C6	–	Y	N	–	–	–	–	–	2	1	1	6	124	0
C7	N	N	N	N	N	N	N	Y	2	1	7	0	0	6
CC	2	2	2	32	16	8	2	64 = 128:128						
A1	X	X												
A2	X	X	X	X	X	X	X							
A3								X						
A4								X						
A5								X						
X1	X	X	X	X	X	X	X							
X2								X						

Fig. 5.2. Unsorted mechanically perfect LIQUID INVESTMENT table.

dashes do not play any role in determining rule uniqueness).
Rule R1 is unique because in –

1. row C4 its Y is different from the R2 N;
2. row C4 its Y is different from the R3 N;
3. row C1 its Y is different from the R4 N;
4. row C2 its Y is different from the R5 N;
5. row C3 its Y is different from the R6 N;
6. row C5 its Y is different from the R7 N;
7. row C7 its N is different from the R8 Y.

We could have said "opposes," "counters," "aligns with," "fails to match," or "is not the same," instead of "is different from."

Having proved R1 unique, we reduce our concern to rules R2–R8. Rule R2 is unique because in its row –

1. C6, Y counters N in R3;
2. C1, Y counters N in R4;
3. C2, Y counters N in R5;
4. C3, Y counters N in R6;
5. C4, N counters Y in R7;
6. C7, N counters Y in R8.

Next, working with the further reduced set R3–R8, rule R3 is unique because in its row —

1. C1, Y counters N in R4;
2. C2, Y counters N in R5;
3. C3, Y counters N in R6;
4. C4, N counters Y in R7;
5. C7, N counters Y in R8.

Working with R4–R8, rule R4 is unique because in its row —

1. C1, N counters Y in R5;
2. C1, N counters Y in R6;
3. C1, N counters Y in R7;
4. C7, N counters Y in R8.

Using set R5–R8, rule R5 is unique because for its condition —

1. C2, N counters Y in R6;
2. C2, N counters Y in R7;
3. C7, N counters Y in R8.

Then, focusing our attention on the remaining unproven rules R6–R8, rule R6 must be unique because in its row —

1. C3 there is an N, but R7 has a Y;
2. C7 there is an N, but R8 has a Y.

And finally, R7 and R8 indicate opposite branching directions in row C7, completing our uniqueness scan.

We have now established that the table in Fig. 5.2 is mechanically perfect. The process may seem somewhat laborious, but one soon develops much proficiency in these procedures. Anyway, the resulting confidence gleaned from the insurance of mechanical perfection is well worth the effort.

5.3. ROW-SORTED TABLE

In Fig. 5.2, we have also included the numerics for the RCM, WDC, and DEL columns. As a brief review, let us look at condition row C3. It contains exactly 4 explicit Ys, 1 explicit N, and 3 dashes as tabulated in the RCM. (Note that each row in the RCM must total 8 — the number of rules.) The dashes in C3 have weights (rule CCs) of 32 in R4, 16 in R5, and 64 in R8, for a total WDC of $32+16+64=112$. The C3, the absolute (unsigned) difference between the explicit RCM Y and N counts, is clearly 3: $DEL=4-1=3$.

Referring to our furcation rule (Section 4.3, we first sort, from top to bottom, in ascending WDCs. In Fig. 5.2, C7 should be placed on top, then all rows will be in ascending sequence reading downward. Since C5 and C6 have equal WDCs, they should be subsorted, top to bottom, in ascending DELs. However, both have identical DELs, so we conclude this portion of our row sorting and go on to check DOMs.

Incidentally, the unsorted table in Fig. 5.2 already contains a row (C7) with no dashes, so no minimum-dash row need be expanded for this purpose. Also, no rules can be combined. R1 and R2 have the same CC and action set, but their condition-answer patterns differ in explicit values in exactly one row, C4. Likewise, R3 and R7, with the same CC, do not have combinable or complementary decision patterns at the same C4 row.

In Fig. 5.3, the only Y (hence all the Ys) in C7 is vertically aligned with dashes in all the other rows. Therefore, C7 dominates C1, C2, C3, C4, C5, and C6 — it is a fell swooper. The only N in C1 vertically aligns with dashes in all the lower rows, so it dominates C2, C3, C4, C5, and C6. The only N in C2 aligns with dashes in C3, C4, C5, and C6, and the only N in C3 aligns with dashes in C4, C5, and C6. (Recall that C1, C2, and C3 are second-level fell swoopers and we

	1	2	3	4	5	6	7	8	DC	WDC	DEL	DOM
7	N	N	N	N	N	N	N	Y	0	0	6	1, 2, 3, 4, 5, 6
1	Y	Y	Y	N	Y	Y	Y	–	1	64	5	2, 3, 4, 5, 6
2	Y	Y	Y	–	N	Y	Y	–	2	96	4	3, 4, 5, 6
3	Y	Y	Y	–	–	N	Y	–	3	112	3	4, 5, 6
4	Y	N	N	–	–	–	Y	–	4	120	0	5, 6
5	Y	–	–	–	–	–	N	–	6	124	0	
6	–	Y	N	–	–	–	–	–	6	124	0	

Fig. 5.3. Row-sorted LIQUID INVESTMENT table.

employed a diagonal of Ns to fit them smoothly into a mechanically perfect pattern.)

In C4, both of its Ns vertically align with dashes in C5 and both of its Ys align with dashes in C6, so C4 dominates C5 and C6.

The one Y in C5 is over a dash in C6, and the one N in C5 is also over a dash in C6. The Y and N in C6 are under dashes. Together, the patterns offer mutual dominance; hence, neither dominates the other.

Practitioners place various arbitrary limitations on citing dominances because of their concerns with different implementation problems. Some examples are as follows:

1. No restrictions (in which case we should have listed C5 as dominating C6).
2. After the initial row sort on WDCs and DELs, for example, determine DOMs by proceeding top to bottom but looking both up and down for vertically aligned dashes, flagging each dash as it is used in establishing a dominance. That is, each – is converted to a $\neq$ when first used. Then –

   a. search upward only to unflagged dashes, or
   b. search (up or down) only to complete sets of unflagged dashes, or
   c. search (up or down) only to sets of dashes, at least one of which is unflagged.

The author's experience indicates that the most general, least arbitrary case, case 1 above (no restrictions), is too permissive, tending to result in tables with conflicting dominances that must later be arbitrarily resolved anyway. The most restrictive case is 2(b) — never reuse any dash under any circumstance. Quite arbitrarily, case 2(b) will be adopted herein because it will create a minimum of problems in later design steps. However, none of the above cases are necessarily right or wrong.

Referring to Fig. 5.3, by the time we started searching for row C5 dominances, all the dashes in the entire table had been flagged. Thus, we suspended our search after C4. Since all rows are above those they dominate (we never had to look upwards for dashes), our row sort is now completed.

In many simple, "clean-cut" tables, the DC and the WDC are executed in top-to-bottom ascending sequence, no re-sorting has to be done to place rows above those they dominate, and furcation proceeds with no complications. However, it's not completely clear what constitutes a simple clean-cut table (unless we have just now indirectly defined it). At least the Fig. 5.3 table appears clean-cut.

5.4. COMPLETELY SORTED TABLE

Remember that we column sort by rows, top to bottom, in a left-to-right YES-NO-DASH sequence. Column sorting C7 yields

```
        8
    7   Y   N   N   N   N   N   N   N
    1   -
    2   -
    3   -
    4   -
    5   -
    6   -
```

and we have uniquely identified rule 8 and filled it in. Next, column sorting C1 results in

	8							4
7	Y	N	N	N	N	N	N	N
1	–	Y	Y	Y	Y	Y	Y	N
2	–							–
3	–							–
4	–							–
5	–							–
6	–							–

and we have uniquely identified the first of our three second-level fell swoopers.

Column sorting C2 gives us

	8						5	4
7	Y	N	N	N	N	N	N	N
1	–	Y	Y	Y	Y	Y	Y	N
2	–	Y	Y	Y	Y	Y	N	–
3	–						–	–
4	–						–	–
5	–						–	–
6	–						–	–

and column sorting C3 gives

	8					6	5	4
7	Y	N	N	N	N	N	N	N
1	–	Y	Y	Y	Y	Y	Y	N
2	–	Y	Y	Y	Y	Y	N	–
3	–	Y	Y	Y	Y	N	–	–
4	–					–	–	–
5	–					–	–	–
6	–					–	–	–

Next, sorting C4, we have

```
         8           6  5  4
  7  Y  N  N  N  N  N  N  N
  1  -  Y  Y  Y  Y  Y  Y  N
  2  -  Y  Y  Y  Y  Y  N  -
  3  -  Y  Y  Y  Y  N  -  -
  4  -  Y  Y  N  N  -  -  -
  5  -              -  -  -
  6  -              -  -  -
```

which failed to uniquely disclose any single rule. Proceeding to C5:

```
         8  1  7     6  5  4
  7  Y  N  N  N  N  N  N  N
  1  -  Y  Y  Y  Y  Y  Y  N
  2  -  Y  Y  Y  Y  Y  N  -
  3  -  Y  Y  Y  Y  N  -  -
  4  -  Y  Y  N  N  -  -  -
  5  -  Y  N  -  -  -  -  -
  6  -  -  -     -  -  -
```

Rules 1 and 7 are singled out. Finally, C6 completes our sort:

```
         8  1  7  2  3  6  5  4
  7  Y  N  N  N  N  N  N  N
  1  -  Y  Y  Y  Y  Y  Y  N
  2  -  Y  Y  Y  Y  Y  N  -
  3  -  Y  Y  Y  Y  N  -  -
  4  -  Y  Y  N  N  -  -  -
  5  -  Y  N  -  -  -  -  -
  6  -  -  -  Y  N  -  -  -
```

Note that completely across any row, there are no repeated Y-N-—sequences, but under each subdivision (as would be clear in a bifurcation) there is such a sequence. For example, under the four Ys in C3 we do have both Ys ahead of the two Ns in C4.

5.5. FLOWCHART IMPLEMENTATION

The completed table is sketched symbolically in Fig. 5.4, where all the conditions and rules have been renumbered for orderly presentation. The condition-matrix bifurcations are as follows:

	1	2	3	4	5	6	7	8
1	Y	N	N	N	N	N	N	N
2	–	Y	Y	Y	Y	Y	Y	N
3	–	Y	Y	Y	Y	Y	N	–
4	–	Y	Y	Y	Y	N	–	–
5	–	Y	Y	N	N	–	–	–
6	–	Y	N	–	–	–	–	–
7	–	–	–	Y	N	–	–	–

In rules 4 and 5, rows 6 and 7, the YN pattern of C7 is below the two dashes of C6. However, by simply eyeballing the matrix, it should be clear that we simply skip over C6 and go right to the testing of C7. Hence, no real difficulty is encountered in the bifurcation, and our table is essentially clean-cut.

Now, with the aid of our bifurcation and the completed table, we get the flowchart readily – "for free." This flowchart, in several forms (4,6), is drawn in Fig. 5.5, and since it represents a complete program, we employ the terminal ellipses for START and STOP.

If we are interested in following through on decision storage and execution of figures of merit, note in Fig. 5.5 that there are 7 stored tests (7 conditions each tested once only). Now assuming all 8 rules are equally likely (ridiculous for the reality of this problem, especially since rule 1 is only executed once, as you leave the store, but the others can all occur many times and GO AGAIN), the average number of tests would be found by studying the number of tests for each rule.

	R1	R2	R3	R4	R5	R6	R7	R8
C1	Y	N	N	N	N	N	N	N
C2	–	Y	Y	Y	Y	Y	Y	N
C3	–	Y	Y	Y	Y	Y	N	–
C4	–	Y	Y	Y	Y	N	–	–
C5	–	Y	Y	N	N	–	–	–
C6	–	Y	N	–	–	–	–	–
C7	–	–	–	Y	N	–	–	–
A1		X		X				
A2		X	X	X	X	X	X	X
A3	X							
A4	X							
A5	X							
X1		X	X	X	X	X	X	X
X2	X							

Fig. 5.4. Completed LIQUID INVESTMENT table.

From our earlier bifurcation, it is clear that R1 requires 1 test (C1), R2 requires 6 tests (C1, C2, C3, C4, C5, and C6), R3, R4, and R5 each require 6, R6 requires 4, R7 requires 3, and R8 requires 2. Thus, the average number of tests per rule is

$$(1+6+6+6+6+4+3+2) \div 8 = 34/8 = 4.25$$

A final thought on the second-level set of fell swoopers, or, in general, on any set of fell swoopers at any level is, Why not put them all together into a single *compound test*? For example, for C1, C2, and C3 in Fig. 5.1, a *single condition* might be, Is the wine a California white varietal, *and* is it from one of the three counties, *and* is it in the 1.5-liter size?

The use of compound tests, using Boolean connectives such as AND and OR, is a somewhat complicated matter of worksheet space, DT clarity, judgment of the designer, and the instruction set of the computer language employed. For instance, does the computer language accommodate Boolean connectives and does it do so with clarity?

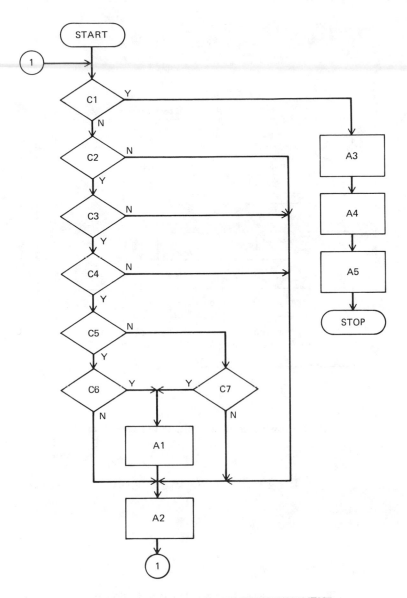

Fig. 5.5(a). Flow diagram for LIQUID INVESTMENT.

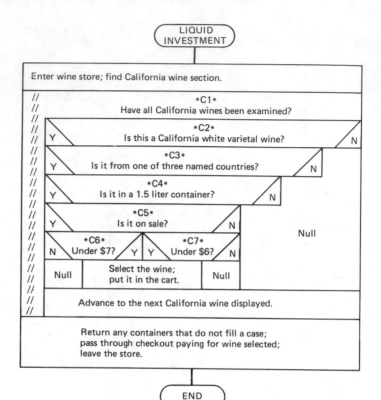

Fig. 5.5(b). Chapin chart for LIQUID INVESTMENT (4,6).

LIQUID INVESTMENT

INPUT

Wine displayed in store
Labels on the displayed wine

OUTPUT

Wine purchased

Fig. 5.5(c). Semicode for LIQUID INVESTMENT (6).

FUNCTIONS

START SELECT LIQUID INVESTMENTS
Enter wine store
Find California wine section
LOOP
EXIT when all California wines examined
   IF wine is a California white varietal
      IF wine is from one of three named counties
         IF wine is in 1.5-liter containers
            If wine is on sale
               IF wine is priced under $7
                  Select the wine
                  Put it in the cart
               END-IF
             ELSE wine is not on sale
               IF wine is priced under $6
                  Select the wine
                  Put it in the cart
               END-IF
            END-IF
         END-IF
      END-IF
   END-IF
   Advance to the next California wine displayed
END-LOOP
Return any containers that do not fill a case
Pass through checkout paying for wine selected
Leave the store
END SELECT LIQUID INVESTMENT

Fig. 5.5(c) Continued

6
Multimodule Decision
Tables

6.1. FUNCTIONAL SPECS FOR STOCKS AND BONDS

We have developed DTs for several individual modules, but we have yet to put together a complete mulitmodule set of DTs. For this purpose we will consider two small illustrations, one called STOCKS & BONDS and the other (treated later in this chapter) called CRAPS DUEL.

For STOCKS & BONDS, the narrative description is given below:

1. We decide to spend the market day trading in either stocks or bonds or nothing, depending on market conditions and our finances. If stocks are low (Dow Jones Industrial Average [DJIA] less than 800), we will pick stocks for the day; if bonds are low (Dow Jones Bond Average [DJBA] less than 80), we will pick bonds; and, if they are both low, we will compare ten times the DJBA to the DJIA to see which is the better buy of the day. We buy nothing if both markets are high.

2. Our selections will be governed by information in either *Standard & Poor's Bond Guide* or *Standard & Poor's Stock Reports,* plus current market prices. Whichever we choose for the day, we will progress sequentially through the *S & P* listings.

3. Our purchases will each be in $2000 or $1000 amounts per security. For the larger purchases, a bond must be rated A,

have a current yield of at least 10%, and a yield to maturity of at least 15%. A stock must have a yield greater than 7% and a growth rate of at least 7%. For the smaller purchases, a grade A bond must have a current yield of at least 10%, and a grade B bond must have a current yield of at least 10% plus a yield to maturity of at least 15%. Grade C bonds will not be purchased, and no more securities will be considered once our cash reserves drop below $2000 or the market closes.

4. Smaller stock purchases will be made either if the growth rate is at least 7% or if the growth rate is at least 5%, but less than 7%, and the yield is greater than 7%. Otherwise, no purchase is made. Also, no stock is purchased if the corporation's debt exceeds its annual net income or if its current price-earnings (PE) ratio is greater than 10.

5. Sales of all holdings of any bond will be made if the current yield is less than 10% or if the bond is rated lower than B. Sales of all holdings of any stock will be made if the yield is 7% or less, or if the debt, PE ratio, or growth rate requirements are failed.

Now, no programmer should attempt to solve a problem until he or she fully understands it — and this problem is no exception. Before getting into details, however, it should be known that this problem is realistic, but it is greatly oversimplified and the particular market averages are in practice adjusted to reflect changing conditions in the market.

A market day, let us assume, is a business day limited by the open hours of the New York exchanges, 10:00 A.M. to 4:00 P.M. Eastern Time. We will also assume that the execution of our DT begins at the opening bell of the market day, and we will choose our day's activity based on the DJIA and DJBA values at the close of the prior market day.

Suppose a bond of the XYZ corporation was listed in the business section of your paper as

$$XYZ \quad 8s97 \quad 13 \quad 60$$

This statement tells us that a transaction took place (probably the last one of the prior business day) in which one party sold some XYZ bonds at a price of 60 (60% of $1000 — the nominal face value of a bond). That is, the transaction took place at $600 per bond. Also, this statement tells us that this bond pays 8% interest a year (0.08 $\times$ $1000 = $80) in two semiannual ("s") installments of $40 each. It also informs us that the bond matures in 1997 at which time it will be redeemed by the issuing XYZ company for about $1000.

Should you have purchased that bond under these conditions, your *current annual yield* would be

$$\$80 \div \$600 = 0.13 = 13\%$$

Assuming this year is 1987, then you would also realize a capital gain of $1000 − $600 = $400 spread over a period of 10 years (1987-1999). Thus, you have an additional "hidden yield" of $400 $\div$ 10 = $40 per year (somewhat oversimplified, that is, not considering compounding effects). Thus your total *yield to maturity* would be about

$$(\$80 + \$40) \div \$600 = 0.2 = 20\%$$

Now suppose the stock of the XYZ corporation was listed in your paper as

$$\text{XYZ} \quad 1 \quad 8 \quad 6 \quad 12\frac{1}{2}$$

This tells us the stock is currently selling at about $12.50 per share and currently pays an annual dividend of $1 (probably in $0.25 quarterly installments, but subject to change up or down at any time). Hence, if you bought this stock at 12½, your expected near-term annual yield would be

$$\$1 \div \$12.50 = 0.08 = 8\%$$

Further, suppose the earnings per share (net corporate earnings over the latest 12 months divided by the total number of outstanding shares) was $2.08. This stock is then said to have a PE ration of

$$\$12.50 \div \$2.08 = 6.$$

Further, suppose that the annual earnings of the XYZ corporation have grown at a more or less steady rate over the past 10 years, from $0.88 per share ten years ago. The ten-year earnings ratio is therefore $2.08 ÷ $0.92 = 2.26, and, in turn, it can be shown that

$$(1 + r) = (2.26)^{1/10}$$

for a compound *annual growth rate* of

$$r = 0.0855 = 8.55\%$$

We will assume that we conduct our business in a brokerage house equipped with advisory service materials (from which we determine quality, debt, long-term earnings and dividends, and so on) and a computer-based display terminal (from which we get up-to-the-minute market prices, latest 12-months' earnings, current yields, PE ratios, and so forth). Incidentally, though not realistic, we will pay or receive spot cash for every transaction we make.

6.2. MODULAR STRUCTURE

After achieving a general understanding of the problem, our next step is to subdivide or modularize the program. Here the principles of function parsing from software engineering give us good guidance (3).

The overall function is to trade in stocks and bonds. The input is the list of current holdings, the DJIA, the DJBA, current prices, bond ratings, bond current yields, bond yield to maturity, stock yield, stock-price growth rate, corporate debt ratio, PE ratio, cash available, time, and business hours. The output indicates how much to buy or sell of which security. Since the controlling data are the two averages, the business hours, the time, and the cash available, the functions that use these data for selecting the major functions to do should be kept in the top module.

This suggests separating out from the other functions the details of handling both the stock and the bond transaction. To support either of these, some accounting work is needed to determine the effects of each transaction on the available cash. This parsing of the functions is summarized in Fig. 6-1.

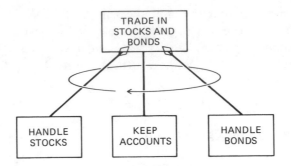

Fig. 6.1. Modular structure for STOCKS & BONDS.

Our chosen structure is shown in Fig. 6.1. We start out the day with the top module, which checks our initial financial status. Then we either close shop for the day (if business looks bad) or enter a loop involving the accounting module and either the BOND module or the STOCK module to guide our day's activities. Either of these two choices keep returning to the top module to ascertain if we still have adequate funds and that the market closing bell has not sounded.

6.3. TRADE MODULE

The TRADE MODULE is almost so simple that we may be able to fill it in, perfectly sorted, on the first pass. What we need to test are the general market conditions and our available cash. Then we either get a bond guide or a set of stock reports, turn to the first entry, and make an appropriate exit. Some of these activities must be subordinate to others.

The TRADE table, including all its numerics, is given in Fig. 6.2. Note that we systematically filled in the condition-entry pattern as for a classical expansion, starting with a column of all Ys and progressing toward a column of all Ns, but exploiting don't-care dashes along the way. The first rule 1 fits a day when both stocks and bonds closed low the market day before, but bonds looked especially good. Likewise, rule 2 fits a generally good day, but stocks look more attractive than bonds.

The dashes in rules 3, 4, and 5 are especially interesting. In rule 3, if stocks are cheap (C2 = Y) but bonds are overpriced (C3 = N), then

TRADE table		R1	R2	R3	R4	R5	R6	M	Y	N	–	WDC	DEL	DOM
C1	TRADING POSSIBLE	Y	Y	Y	Y	Y	N	2	5	1	0	0	4	C2, C3, C4
C2	DJIA < 800	Y	Y	Y	N	N	–	2	3	2	1	8	1	C4
C3	DJBA < 80	Y	Y	N	Y	N	–	2	3	2	1	8	1	C4
C4	(10 × DJBA) < DJIA	Y	N	–	–	–	–	2	1	1	4	14	0	
	CC	1	1	2	2	2	8 = 16:16							
A1	UPDATE THE AVERAGES	X	X	X	X	X								
A2	CALL HANDLE BONDS	X			X									
A3	CALL HANDLE STOCKS		X	X										
A4	CALL ACCOUNTING	X	X	X	X									
X1	GO AGAIN	X	X	X	X									
X2	STOP					X	X							

Fig. 6.2. TRADE table.

C4 could only have a NO answer — the C4 dash is an *-type exclusive don't-care (recall Section 2.5 on don't cares). In rule 4, if stocks are expensive but bonds are cheap, C4 could only have a YES answer — the C4 dash is a $-type exclusive don't-care. And in rule 5, if both stocks and bonds are overpriced, we do not care which is better — the C4 dash is an I-type, an inclusive don't care. Thus, the lower part of the condition-entry matrix could have been patterned as

	1	2	3	4	5
C2	Y	Y	Y	N	N
C3	Y	Y	N	Y	N
C4	Y	N	*	$	I

The DOM column also illustrates an interesting dash situation. The two Ns in row C2, rules 4 and 5, are vertically matched by dashes in C4, so C2 dominates C4. Also, the two Ns in row C3, rules 3 and 5, are vertically matched by dashes, so C3 also dominates C4.

When C2 dominance over C4 was established, we (mentally or on a scratch pad) flagged the last two dashes in row C4 (rules 4 and 5). Then, when checking for C3 dominance over C4, we found one of the needed dashes (rule 5) already flagged, and so we could not use it.

The reader should be advised that this is a quite arbitrary method. Some practitioners consider a table to be "pathological" unless all dashes are flagged at least once. Thus, if we had permitted reuse, C3 would have been shown to dominate C4 in Fig. 6.2, and all three dashes would have been flagged (used in dominance determinations) at least once.

A bifurcation of the decision matrix

	1	2	3	4	5	6
C1	Y	Y	Y	Y	Y	N
C2	Y	Y	Y	N	N	–
C3	Y	Y	N	Y	N	–
C4	Y	N	–	–	–	–

readily gives the flowchart of Fig. 6.3.

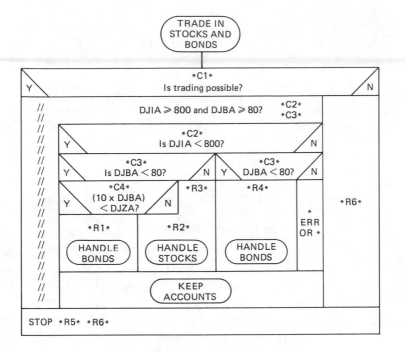

Fig. 6.3. Chapin chart for TRADE table.

Note the action section exits are a GO AGAIN and a STOP in Figs. 6.2 and 6.3.

6.4. ACCOUNTING

The ACCOUNTING table is a little easier than TRADE table to do perfectly in a single pass. All we have is a positive diagonal of three fell swoopers — MARKET CLOSED, TRANSACTION AWAITING ACCOUNTING, and CASH BALANCE < $2000 — and its accompanying all-NO column. The DT is shown in Fig. 6.4 (note the RETURN exit) and the matching flowchart in Fig. 6.5.

The ACCOUNTING table illustrates two important practices in DT preparation. One is the need for testing a condition whose value is not known until after the actions have been taken. The GO AGAIN and C2 fell swooper in Fig. 6.4 is one way of handling this situation. Another way is to reverse a condition so that Y may be used instead

ACCOUNTING table		R1	R2	R3	R4	M	Y	N	–	WDC	DEL	DOM
C1	MARKET CLOSED	Y	N	N	N	2	1	3	0	0	2	C2, C3
C2	TRANSACTION AWAITING ACCOUNTING	–	Y	N	N	2	1	2	1	4	1	C3
C3	CASH BALANCE < $2000	–	–	Y	N	2	1	1	2	4	0	
	CC	4	2	1	1 = 8:8							
A1	UPDATE CASH BALANCE		X									
A2	SET TO TRADING POSSIBLE				X							
A3	SET TO TRADING NOT POSSIBLE	X		X								
X1	GO AGAIN		X									
X2	RETURN	X		X	X							

Fig. 6.4. ACCOUNTING table.

of N and N instead of Y in sorting the DT. Condition C2 shows one way of handling this situation (instead of ACCOUNTING DONE, for example).

A practical aspect of the interaction of DT condition dominance and software engineering appears in Fig. 6.5. In software engineering, the third parsing guideline is dominant over the second, and the fourth over both the second and third in the basic set (3). This precept is used in pulling out the iteration and placing it first in Fig. 6.5.

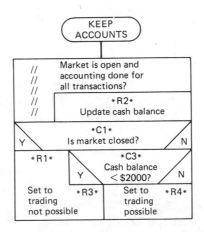

Fig. 6.5. Chapin chart for ACCOUNTING table.

6.5. BOND TABLE

The BOND table is shown in final form in Fig. 6.6. Observe that we had three quality ratings, A, B, and C, so an extended entry was appropriate for C1, giving a modulus of 3 and resulting in a moduli product of 3 X 2 X 2 X 2 = 24. The rules of most interest are 1, 2, and 5. In rule 1, the bond has all three desirable features – high quality, high current yield, and high yield to maturity – so we buy the larger amount. In rule 2, the yield to maturity is not as high, and in rule 5, the quality is down one grade, so we only buy $1000 worth.

In the RCM it should be noted that in row C1, blank spaces rather than zeros were placed in the N and Y columns. Zeros would have implied that N and Y were potentially valid quality ratings. Similarly, blanks appear in the C2, C3, and C4 rows of the RCM in the A, B, and C columns since C2, C3, and C4 can only have Y and N answers.

A furcation (not simply a bifurcation since C1 must be trifurcated) of the decision matrix:

	1	2	3	4	5	6	7	8	9	10
C1	A	A	A	A	B	B	B	B	C	C
C2	Y	Y	N	N	Y	Y	N	N	–	–
C3	–	–	Y	N	–	–	Y	N	Y	N
C4	Y	N	–	–	Y	N	–	–	–	–

readily yields the flowchart of Fig. 6.7.

Should we be interested in decision storage and execution measures, note from Fig. 6.7 that there are 6 diagonal mark-off rectangle tests that must be stored (three of the conditions stored twice).

From Fig. 6.6, it is clear that rules 1 through 8 each require 3 tests, while rules 9 and 10 each need the execution of 2 tests to reach their action sequences. Thus, assuming all rules are equally likely to occur, the average number of tests per execution pass is

$$(8 \times 3) + (2 \times 2) \div 10 = 28/10 = 2.8$$

HANDLE BONDS	R1	2	3	4	5	6	7	8	9	10	M	WDC	A	B	C	Y	N	-	DEL	DOM
C1 QUALITY RATING	A	A	A	A	B	B	B	B	C	C	3	0	4	4	2				2	C2, C3, C4
C2 CURRENT YIELD > 10%	Y	Y	N	N	Y	Y	N	N	-	-	2	8				4	4	2	0	C3, C4
C3 HOLDING NOW	-	-	Y	Y	-	-	Y	Y	N	N	2	8				3	3	4	0	C4
C4 YIELD TO MATURITY > 15%	Y	N	-	-	Y	N	-	-	-	-	2	16				2	2	6	0	
CC	2	2	2	2	2	2	2	2	4	4	4=24:24									
A1 BUY $2000 WORTH	X																			
A2 BUY $1000 WORTH		X			X															
A3 SELL HOLDINGS			X			X			X											
A4 REPORT TRANSACTION		X	X		X	X	X	X	X	X										
A5 TURN TO NEXT BOND LISTING		X	X	X	X	X	X	X	X	X										
X1 RETURN	X	X	X	X	X	X	X	X	X	X										

Fig. 6.6. BOND table.

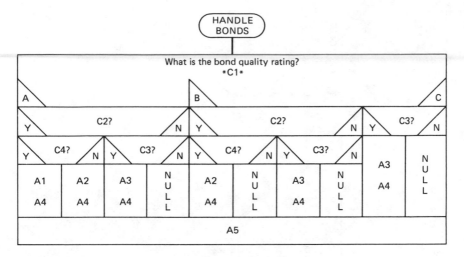

Fig. 6.7. Chapin chart for BOND table.

6.6. STOCK TABLE

The STOCK routine is very similar to the BOND routine. Thus, relatively little comment is needed.

Like the quality rating in the BOND routine, the growth rate in the STOCK routine is three-valued. Namely, the growth rate can be $<5\%$, between 5% and 7%, and $\geq 7\%$, which are coded in C4 of Fig. 6.8 as 1, 2, and 3, respectively. Again an extended form was used, with a modulus of 3 leading to a moduli product of $2 \times 2 \times 2 \times 3 \times 2 = 48$.

A point of interest in the STOCK table is that C1, C2 and C3 are not quite swoopers in spite of the positive near-diagonal of Ys followed by an expanded set of all-NO columns. Note that the early recognition of various levels of dominances by any true fell swoopers helps to obtain correct row sorting early during the design of a DT. In Fig. 6.8, note how the lack of C2-C3 dominance causes a different organization of the tests in the Chapin charts. Since the actions are repetitious, the common implementation practice is to invoke them by a CALL or a PERFORM or a DO.

A furcation of the condition matrix:

	HANDLE STOCKS	R1	R2	R3	R4	R5	R6	R7	R8	R9	R10	R11	M	Y	N	1	2	3	–	WDC	DEL	DOM
C1	DEBT > ANNUAL NET INCOME	Y	Y	N	N	N	N	N	N	N	N	N	2	2	9					0	7	C2,C3,C4,C5
C2	HOLDING THE STOCK	Y	N	Y	Y	Y	Y	N	N	N	–	–	2	4	4				3	6	0	C4,C5
C3	PE RATIO > 10	–	–	Y	N	N	N	N	N	N	N	N	2	2	7				2	24	5	C4,C5
C4	GROWTH RATE CODE	–	–	1	1	2	–	1	2	2	3	3	3			2	3	2	4	36	1	C5
C5	YIELD > 7% CC	–	–	–	–	N	–	–	N	Y	Y	Y	2	2	3				6	40	1	
	CC	12	12	6	2	1	6	2	1	2	2	2	2=48:48									
A1	BUY $2000										X											
A2	BUY $1000											X										
A3	SELL HOLDINGS	X		X	X	X																
A4	REPORT TRANSACTION	X		X	X	X	X	X	X	X	X	X										
A5	TURN TO NEXT REPORT			X	X	X	X	X	X	X	X	X										
X1	RETURN	X	X	X	X	X	X	X	X	X	X	X										

Fig. 6.8. STOCK table.

	R1	R2	R3	R4	R5	R6	R7	R8	R9	R10	R11
C1	Y	Y	N	N	N	N	N	N	N	N	N
C2	Y	N	Y	Y	Y	N	N	N	–	–	–
C3	–	–	Y	N	N	Y	N	N	N	N	N
C4	–	–	–	1	2	–	1	2	2	3	3
C5	–	–	–	–	N	–	–	N	Y	Y	N

guides us in making the flowchart of Fig. 6.9.

6.7. CRAPS DUEL PROGRAM

The sporting game of craps is played with a pair of dice. Each die is a cube with 6 faces, the various faces containing 1, 2, 3, 4, 5, and 6 dots. The score when rolling a pair of dice is the face-up sum of the dot counts.

According to the dictionary definition of craps, the crapshooter wins if the first roll yields a score of 7 or 11 and loses if the first roll

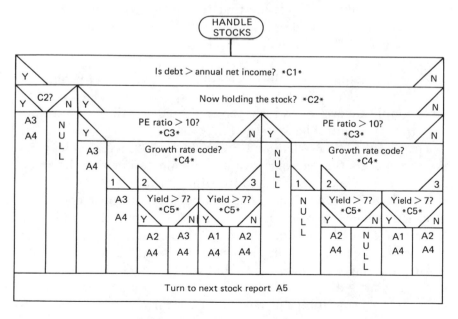

Fig. 6.9. Chapin chart for STOCK table.

yields a score of 2, 3, or 12. Otherwise, the crapshooter continues to roll until a point is made (the score of the first roll is matched). However, the crapshooter loses if a 7 is rolled before a point is made, but wins if a point is made before rolling a 7. This game is almost fair — the crapshooter has a probability of winning of slightly greater than 49%.

We are going to invent a game which is not intended to be fair (only interesting and fun, we hope), called CRAPS DUEL. This game is played by two players, 1 and 2. The functional specs are listed below:

1. Two players, 1 and 2, armed with a pair of dice, are to compete for a prize.
2. Player 1's turn consists of a limit of 6 games of craps. During the turn, player 1 wins the prize by winning three successive games of craps.
3. Player 2's turn consists of a limit of 10 games. During the turn, player 2 wins the prize by losing four successive games.
4. The two players alternate taking turns until one wins the prize. Player 1 gets the first turn if, and only if, the day of the month is odd or it is winter, unless the birthday of player 2 occurs during the current season.

We will interpret the solution to this problem as a program with five unique modules as pictured in Fig. 6.10. The START PLAY table simply determines which player should get the first turn and then transfers control back to the PLAY table.

The PLAY FOR 3 WINS and PLAY FOR 4 LOSSES tables guide the two players through one turn and culminate in either the acceptance of the prize or a transfer to the other player.

The SHOOT A GAME table guides either player through the playing of exactly one game of craps and then returns control to whichever table invoked it after setting a WIN SWITCH either ON or OFF. This routine requires that the player invoking it must make the first roll before it is invoked, to prevent the SHOOT A GAME table from having to start with an action (a matter discussed later). Here we still are restricting condition stubs to conditions only, and action stubs to actions only.

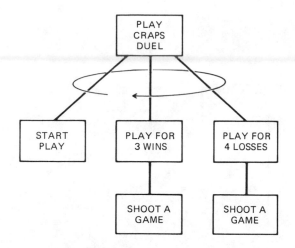

Fig. 6.10. Modular structure for CRAPS DUEL.

The two players' tables must maintain counters that keep track of how many games have been played and how many successive wins (or losses) have accumulated during the execution of a turn.

6.8. CRAPS DUEL MODULES

The DT for the top module of the hierarchy has to provide actions for doing each of the three second-level DTs. The DT must also provide for iteration (repetition) until the prize has been won. Fig. 6.11 offers a DT for these activities.

A comparison of Fig. 6.11 with Fig. 6.12 reveals an important limitation of decision tables. Clearly, when only sequential action is needed, no tests are needed. Hence, Fig. 6.12 shows fewer tests of conditions than does Fig. 6.11. This is because a DT requires an explicit statement of conditions (such as C1), whereas a chart, be it an ANSI flowchart or a Chapin chart, permits sometimes an implicit recognition of some conditions.

The START PLAY table is shown in Fig. 6.13, and its matching Chapin chart, in Fig. 6.14. The only feature of interest is its condition-entry matrix, which looks like a perfect fell swooper. Hence, it should be clear that not all diagonal patterns represent a set of fell swoopers or a set of mutually exclusive conditions.

PLAY CRAPS DUEL		R1	R2	R3	R4	R5	R6	M	Y	N	–	WDC	DEL	DOM
C1	DUEL BEING STARTED	Y	Y	Y	N	N	N	2	3	3	0	0	0	C2,C3,C4,C5
C2	NO FIRST PLAYER CHOSEN	Y	N	N	–	–	–	2	1	2	3	16	1	C4
C3	PRIZE WON	–	–	–	Y	N	N	2	1	2	3	16	1	C5
C4	3 WINS GOES FIRST	–	Y	N	–	–	–	2	1	1	4	24	0	
C5	3 WINS HAD LAST TURN	–	–	–	–	Y	N	2	1	1	4	24	0	
	CC	8	4	4	8	4	4=32:32							
A1	CALL START PLAY	X												
A2	CALL PLAY FOR 3 WINS		X				X							
A3	CALL PLAY FOR 4 LOSSES			X		X								
X1	GO AGAIN	X	X	X		X	X							
X2	STOP				X									

Fig. 6.11. PLAY CRAPS DUEL table.

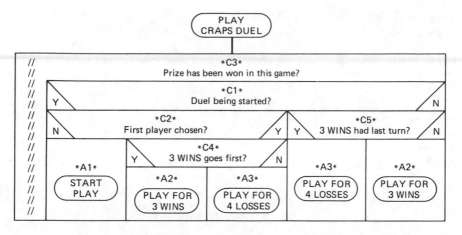

Fig. 6.12. Chapin chart for PLAY CRAPS DUEL.

	START PLAY table	1	2	3	4	M	Y	N	–	WDC	DEL	DOM
C1	PLAYER 2'S BIRTHDAY IN SEASON	Y	N	N	N	2	1	3	0	0	2	C2,C3
C2	DAY OF MONTH ODD	–	Y	N	N	2	1	2	1	4	1	C3
C3	WINTER	–	–	Y	N	2	1	1	2	6	0	
	CC	4	2	1	1 = 8:8							
A1	SET PLAY FOR 3 WINS FIRST		X	X								
A2	SET PLAY FOR 4 LOSSES FIRST	X			X							
X1	RETURN	X	X	X	X							

Fig. 6.13. START PLAY table for CRAPS DUEL.

Fig. 6.14. Chapin chart for START PLAY for CRAPS DUEL.

	SHOOT A GAME	1	2	3	4	5	6	7	M	Y	N	–	WDC	DEL	DOM
C1	FIRST ROLL	Y	Y	Y	Y	N	N	N	2	4	3	0	0	1	C2,C4,C5
C2	SCORE 2, 3, OR 12	Y	N	N	N	–	–	–	2	1	3	3	16	2	C3,C5
C3	SCORE 7	–	Y	N	N	Y	N	N	2	2	4	1	8	2	
C4	SCORE SAME AS FIRST	–	–	–	–	–	Y	N	2	1	1	5	24	0	
C5	SCORE 11	–	–	Y	N	–	–	–	2	1	1	5	28	0	
	CC	8	4	2	2	8	4	4=32:32							
A1	TURN OFF WIN SWITCH	X				X									
A2	TURN ON WIN SWITCH		X	X			X								
A3	ROLL DICE				X			X							
A4	SAVE FIRST ROLL SCORE				X										
X1	GO AGAIN				X			X							
X2	RETURN	X	X	X		X	X								

Fig. 6.15. SHOOT A GAME table.

The SHOOT A GAME table is illustrated in Fig. 6.15, and its matching Chapin chart, in Fig. 6.16. Note that the WDC is *not* sorted perfectly in top-down ascending sequence. In this table it was necessary to make a final row change after the initial WDC row sort in order to place C2 above C3, which it dominates. Also note that C2 would have dominated C4 because of its 3 Ns and the C4 dashes in

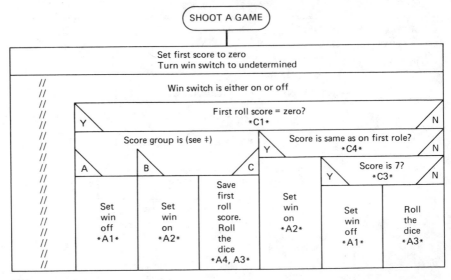

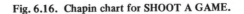

‡Score groups are:
A — 2 or 3 or 12 (C2)
B — 7 or 11 (C3, C5)
C — 4 or 5 or 6 or 8 or 9 or 10

Fig. 6.16. Chapin chart for SHOOT A GAME.

rules 2, 3, and 4, had these dashes not already been flagged by the Ys in C1. In addition, C2 could have dominated C4 because of the C2 Y matching the C4 dash in rule 1 had this dash not already been flagged.

Observe that this table requires that the calling table execute the first roll of the dice to avoid an action preceding C1. Otherwise, this table plays one complete game of craps, the first test, C1, simply dividing the table into first-roll and later-roll portions.

Figure 6.16 takes advantage of the implied logical exclusive OR relationship between the columns of a decision table in assigning score groups. The Chapin chart also gives the previously noted dominance to the iterated actions and uses the all-No status in the DT to resequence the tests shown on the right hand side of the chart — the main path through the body of the iterated loop body.

The PLAY FOR 3 WINS table is pictured in Fig. 6.17, and its matching Chapin chart, in Fig. 6.18. Note that it also required a final row-sort step to place C3 above C4, which it dominates (and the row sort is no longer a perfect WDC sequence). Also observe that there is one fell swooper, C1, which leads to the turn-initialization rule, rule 1.

A careful study of this module will also reveal that it favors minimum storage rather than minimum execution time. Unless player 1 wins during a particular turn, player 1 will play out a full set of 6 games of craps even if there is not value to do so. For example, if player 1 has lost at least 2 of the first 4 games, including the 4th, there is no chance to win the prize during this turn with only 2 games left, but player 1 plays them anyway. Recall that player 1 can win the duel only by winning three successive games of craps during a single turn.

This execution waste could be avoided by adding several additional tests (which add to execution time!) that determine if it is still possible to win the prize at any point after a play count of 4, but that would increase storage requirements and complicate the DT.

The routine for player 2 is essentially identical to that for player 1 except for the number of games allowed (10 instead of 6) and the number of successive hits (4 losses instead of 3 wins). Hence, the general scheme presented in Figs. 6.19 and 6.20 matches the scheme presented in Figs. 6.17 and 6.18.

PLAY FOR 3 WINS table	1	2	3	4	5	6	M	Y	N	–	WDC	DEL	DOM
C1	BEGINNING OF TURN	Y	N	N	N	N	N	2	1	5	0	0	4	C2,C3,C4
C2	WIN SWITCH ON	–	Y	Y	Y	N	N	2	3	2	1	8	1	C3
C3	WIN COUNTER HOLDS A 2	–	Y	N	N	–	–	2	1	2	3	12	1	C4
C4	PLAY COUNTER HOLDS A6	–	–	Y	N	Y	N	2	2	2	2	10	0	
	CC	8	2	2	1	1	2	2=16:16						
A1	SET PLAY COUNTER TO 0	X												
A2	SET WIN COUNTER TO 0	X					X							
A3	INCREMENT WIN COUNTER BY 1				X									
A4	ROLL DICE	X			X		X							
A5	CALL SHOOT A GAME	X			X		X							
A6	INCREMENT PLAY COUNTER BY 1	X			X		X							
A7	RECEIVE PRIZE		X											
X1	GO AGAIN	X			X	X								
X2	RETURN		X	X		X								

Fig. 6.17. PLAY FOR 3 WINS table.

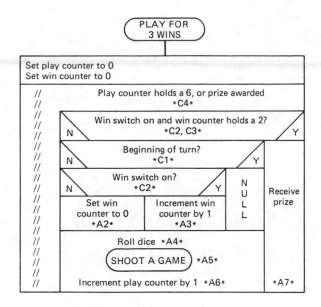

Fig. 6.18. Chapin charts for PLAY FOR 3 WINS.

PLAY FOR 4 LOSSES table	1	2	3	4	5	6	M	Y	N	–	WDC	DEL	DOM
C1 BEGINNING OF TURN	Y	N	N	N	N	N	2	1	5	0	0	4	C2,C3,C4
C2 WIN SWITCH OFF	–	Y	Y	Y	N	N	2	3	2	1	8	1	C3
C3 LOSE COUNTER HOLD A 3	–	Y	N	N	–	–	2	1	2	3	12	1	C4
C4 PLAY COUNTER HOLD A 10	–	–	Y	N	Y	N	2	2	2	2	10	0	
CC	8	2	1	1	2	2=16:16							
A1 SET PLAY COUNTER TO 0	X												
A2 SET LOSE COUNTER TO 0	X					X							
A3 INCREMENT LOSE COUNTER BY 1				X									
A4 ROLL DICE	X			X									
A5 CALL SHOOT A GAME	X			X		X							
A6 INCREMENT PLAY COUNTER BY 1	X			X		X							
A7 RECEIVE PRIZE		X											
X1 GO AGAIN	X			X		X							
X2 RETURN		X	X		X								

Fig. 6.19. PLAY FOR 4 LOSSES table.

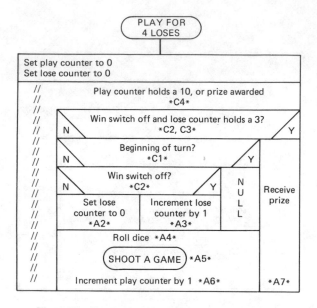

Fig. 6.20. Chapin chart for PLAY FOR 4 LOSSES.

7
Some Interesting Tables

7.1. DAILY INTAKE

On October 3, 1974, the author was informed by this physician that, along with a score of other ailments, he now possessed a duodenal ulcer. With many new restrictions now imposed on this daily intake of food, drink, and medicine, the problem of what to do when became a little too complex for ordinary memory (on top of trying to do a day's work). Thus, he (naturally) developed a decision table to guide his daily intake requirements. Apparently, the physician was uneducated in the intricacies of a DT and left the author to his own devices.

The resulting self-to-self table is illustrated, with all its numerics, in Fig. 7.1. Here is an example of subsorting on ascending DELs. Note that C2 and C3 have equal WDCs of 64. However, their DELs are 0 and 4, respectively. Also, if the tabulated DOMs are studied carefully, it will be found that every dash is flagged exactly once.

Moreover, it is interesting to note that if dashes were not flagged (could be reused), then C2 would dominate C3, C4, C5, C6, and C7 with either its one Y or its one N. And, conversely, C3, C4, C5, C6, and C7 would each dominate C2 — again both on their Y and N portions. In this event we would have quite a set of conflicting dominances that would have to be resolved arbitrarily. By flagging dashes when first used, we avoid this later conflict.

While this DT appears to lead to an infinite loop (always exits with a GO AGAIN), an interrupt occurred after about eight weeks when it was discovered that the ulcer was completely cured! This is termed *event-driven* action; a fell swooper "cured" could have been used.

DAILY INTAKE table	1	2	3	4	5	6	7	8	M	Y	N	–	WDC	DEL	DOM
C1 7 AM	Y	Y	N	N	N	N	N	N	2	2	6	0	0	4	2,3,4,5,6,7
C2 MORNING LECTURE	Y	N	–	–	–	–	–	–	2	1	1	6	64	0	4,5,6,7
C3 8,9,11 AM, 1,2,4,5,7,8,9 PM	–	–	Y	N	N	N	N	N	2	1	5	2	64	4	4,5,6,7
C4 10 AM, 3 PM	–	–	–	Y	–	N	N	N	2	1	4	3	96	3	5,6,7
C5 12 NOON	–	–	–	–	Y	N	N	N	2	1	3	4	112	2	6,7
C6 6 PM	–	–	–	–	–	Y	N	N	2	1	2	5	120	1	7
C7 10 PM	–	–	–	–	–	–	Y	N	2	1	1	6	124	0	7
CC	32	32	32	16	8	4	2	2	2 = 128:128						
A1 2 VITAMIN/MINERAL TABLETS	X	X													
A2 1 VALIUM TABLET (5MG)		X													
A3 2 BENTYL-20 TABLETS	X	X													
A4 3 ASPIRIN TABLETS	X	X													
A5 2 TEASPOONS ANTACID (800MG)			X	X											
A6 SPECIAL EYE DROPS	X	X			X	X	X								
A7 6 OZ. SKIM MILK				X	X										
A8 MILK TOAST (1 SLICE)	X	X													
A9 HALF LOW-FAT CHEESE SANDWICH					X										
A10 1 BANANA (SMALL)					X	X									
A11 4 OZ. EGG SUBSTITUTE						X									
A12 LOW-FAT COTTAGE CHEESE						X									
A13 GELATIN (NO ADDITIVES)						X	X								
A14 LARGE GLASS WATER							X								
X1 GO AGAIN	X	X	X	X	X	X	X	X							

Fig. 7.1. DAILY INTAKE table.

7.2. SPLIT PERSONALITY

The partially decomposed decision matrix of a particular MEDT is sketched in Fig. 7.2. This table has a "split personality" — its (plain) dash counts and its weighted dash counts (WDCs) do not track in sequence. The two numeric columns are

–	WDC
0	0
1	2
3	6
2	8

so the WDC is in sequence, but the unweighted count is not. Such tables are frequently not well behaved or clean cut. Another interesting and somewhat suspicious feature is that there are no dominances at all!

In any event, after applying all our furcation guide rules (Section 4.3), the furcation breaks down in two regions. The lower central submatrix formed by the intersection of rules 6–12 and rows C3–C4 does not yet furcate, and the lower right submatrix formed by the intersection of rules 13–22 and rows C2–C4 is still out of order.

In general, the furcation guide rules should all be re-applied at each subdivision during the decomposition of an entire table. That is, the overall table is furcated along the top row only. Then each exposed lower subtable is treated as a full table in its own right: its numerics are calculated, another row and column sorting takes place, and each is furcated along its top row only, to get new subsubtables, and so on.

The normal and practical procedure is to attempt to sort the table (as we have been doing) so that it will furcate in one pass. When, and only when, a one-pass attempt fails (as it did in this example), do we "pull out" subtables and re-sort them. Generally these subtables are small and simple enough to be re-sorted strictly by eyeballing rather than by formally developing all the numerics and applying all the regular steps.

	1	2	3	4	5	6	7	8	9	10	11	12	13	14	15	16	17	18	19	20	21	22
C1	Y	Y	Y	Y	Y	Y	Y	Y	Y	Y	Y	Y	N	N	N	N	N	N	N	N	N	N
C2	Y	Y	Y	Y	Y	Y	N	N	N	N	N	N	Y	Y	Y	Y	N	N	N	N	N	–
C3	Y	Y	Y	Y	Y	Y	Y	Y	Y	N	N	N	N	N	N	N	N	N	N	–	–	–
C4	–	A	B	C	D	B	C	D	B	C	D	A	C	B	C	A	D	A	C	D	–	B
CC	4	1	1	1	1	1	1	1	1	1	1	2	1	1	1	1	2	1	1	1	2	2

NOT FURCATED   NOT FURCATED $2 = 32:32$

	M	A	B	C	D	Y	N	–	WDC	DEL	DOM
C1	2					12	10	0	0	2	
C2	2					10	11	1	2	1	
C3	2					9	10	3	6	1	NONE
C4	4	4	5	6	5				8	8	

Fig. 7.2. A "split-personality" table – partially furcated.

Each subtable, just like a full table, must have at least one row, including the top row, free of dashes. For the left subtable in Fig. 7.2, C4 is "solid," so we simply invert C3 and C4 and place C4 in sequence, yielding

	12	6	9	7	10	8	11
C4	A	B	B	C	C	D	D
C3	–	Y	N	Y	N	Y	N

which furcated very easily.

For the right subtable in Fig. 7.2, all three rows contain a dash. So we take the C2/R22 dash (C2 being the sum smallest CC row in this subtable) and expand it to a separate Y and N, creating rules 22a and 22b. Also, it soon becomes apparent that we will again have to invert C3 and C4. Our subtable now looks like

	16	22a	14	13	15	17	18	22b	19	20	21
C2	Y	Y	Y	Y	Y	Y	N	N	N	N	N
C4	A	B	B	C	C	D	A	B	C	D	–
C3	–	Y	N	Y	N	–	Y	Y	Y	Y	N

but its lower-right portion (the intersection of rules 18, 22b, 19, 20, and 21 with conditions C3 and C4) is still not furcated.

Pulling out this final sub-submatrix and reinverting C3 and C4, we get

	18	22b	19	20	21
C3	Y	Y	Y	Y	N
C4	A	B	C	D	–

and so our entire table is finally in ready implementation order.

Observe that throughout the decomposition process, the dash-count sequence (C1, C2, C4, and C3) conflicted with the WDC sequence (C1, C2, C3, and C4). Some rules (1, 2, 3, 4, 5, 6, 18, 19, 20, 21, and 22b) nicely followed the WDC sequence, but in the rest

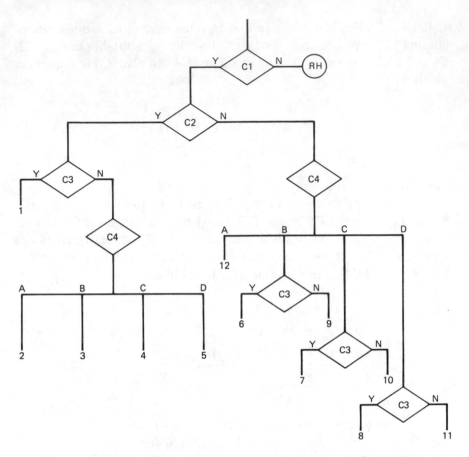

Fig. 7.3. Decision tree for left half of "split-personality" table.

of the rules we find C4 ahead of C3. This conflict is evident in a decision tree implementation drawn in Figs. 7.3 and 7.4.

7.3. INCOMPLETE TABLE

An "incomplete" table is given in Fig. 7.5. Clearly it is not mechanically perfect — 8 rules are missing. However, suppose it *is* physically perfect. That is, it contains all the decision patterns that can possibly occur physically — all missing rules are claimed to be impossible combinations that chose to live dangerously and are "can't-happens."

In this event we can, if we treat it as a complete table, develop its numerics (as we did in Fig. 7.5), and then try to decompose it. Note

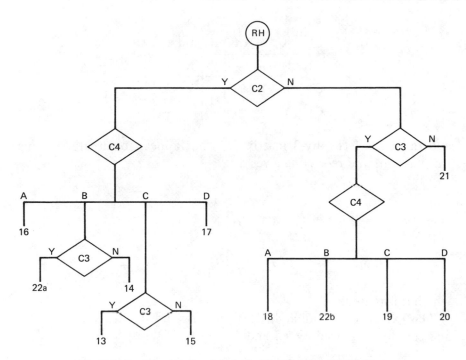

Fig. 7.4. Decision tree for right half of "split-personality" table.

	1	2	3	4	5	6	7	M	A	B	C	Y	N	–	WDC	DEL	DOM
C1	A	A	A	B	B	C	C	3	3	2	2				0	0	1	C4
C2	N	–	–	Y	N	N	N	2				1	4	2	6	3	C3
C3	N	Y	N	–	Y	Y	N	2				3	3	1	4	0	
C4	Y	–	N	–	–	–	N	2				1	2	4	12	1	
CC	1	4	2	4	2	2	1 = 16:24

Fig. 7.5. An "incomplete" table.

that it is not in either dash or WDC sequence because of a dominance (C2 dominates C3).

A furcation attempt yields

	1	2	3	4	5	6	7
C1	A	A	A	B	B	C	C
C2	N	–	–	Y	N	N	N
C3	N	Y	N	–	Y	Y	N
C4	Y	–	N	–	–	–	N

and the lower-left 3-by-3 matrix does not appear to furcate. Pulling this part out and re-sorting gives us

	2	1	3
C3	Y	N	N
C4	–	Y	N
C2	–	N	–

which is furcated.

The extraneous (unmatched) Y and Ns are exclusive don't-cares and could be replaced by a $ and *'s (31 p. 16), respectively, yielding

	1	2	3	4	5	6	7
C1	A	A	A	B	B	C	C
C2				Y	N	*	*
C3				–	$	Y	N
C4				–	–	–	*

and

	2	1	3
C3	Y	N	N
C4	–	Y	N
C2	–	*	–

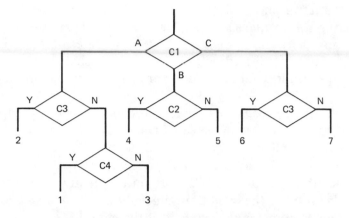

Fig. 7.6. Decision tree for the "incomplete" table.

and we have learned to treat an * or a $ as a dash (need not be tested), so our decomposition is concluded as pictured in Fig. 7.6.

Some practitioners and processors employ what is called an ELSE rule. An ELSE rule is made the very last rule and it contains no entries in the condition entry part (the upper half of the rule is left blank), though it may contain action entries and certainly it needs an exit. It is a catchall, and its actions (or at least its exit) tell what should happen if none of the preceding detailed rules apply.

An ELSE rule could be an added rule for our "incomplete" table of Fig. 7.5. In this event, it automatically picks up the 8 missing rules (and is given a CC=8). Perhaps none of these rules (the simple rules "hidden" in the ELSE rule) *should* occur, but maybe they *could* occur by accident or malfunction. Our ELSE rule would then become an *error* rule and the action might be an error message before a return.

7.4. DETERMINING MISSING RULES

Now suppose that our "incomplete" table of Fig. 7.5 is truly incomplete and we wish to discover and list the missing rules. The easiest procedure is to parse (furcate) the table from top to bottom, one condition at a time, and calculate the successive RCM for each part. The shortages describe the missing rules.

An alternative and more formal procedure uses a weighted RCM for creating rules with as large a CC as possible. Then, we can always expand any resulting complex rule that is determined to lead to different action sets for different values of its dashes.

In this procedure, our main tools for seeking out missing rules are:

1. A dash represents all values of its condition row equally. Each value is weighted by an equal fraction of the rule column CC.
2. Every explicit entry is weighted by the CC of its rule column.
3. Every final and complete row must have every one of its possible condition values represented equally in its totals.
4. The total of the condition values for every final and complete row must match the product of the moduli.
5. Every rule, old or added, must be unique.

We will now make up a *weighted* row count matrix (WRCM), which contains only explicit values for our incomplete table. In effect, all our dashes have been converted to explicits.

	1	2	3	4	5	6	7	WRCM				
								A	B	C	Y	N
C1	A	A	A	B	B	C	C	7	6	3		
C2	N	–	–	Y	N	N	N				7	9
C3	N	Y	N	–	Y	Y	N				10	6
C4	Y	–	N	–	–	–	N				7	9
CC	1	4	2	4	2	2	1					

To see how we filled in this WRCM, in row C1 there are 3 As weighted 1 (CC=1) in rule 1, 4 (CC=4) in rule 2, and 2 (CC=2) in rule 3. Thus, 7 As are represented in row C1. Similarly for the B and C counts. If we had a complete table, the A, B, and C counts would each be 8, for a grand total of 24 — the moduli product.

In row C2, rule 1 gives us 1 N (CC=1), rule 2 gives us 2 Ns (CC=4, but this dash represents 2 Ys and 2 Ns), rule 3 gives us 1 N (CC=2, but this dash gives us 1 Y and 1 N), rule 4 gives only Ys (CC=4 of them), rule 5 gives us 2 Ns (CC=2), rule 6 gives 2 Ns (CC=2), and rule 7 gives us but 1 N (CC=1), for an N count of

$$1+2+1+0+2+2+1 = 9.$$

A similar determination yields the Y count of 7 and the Y and N counts in rows C3 and C4. If this table were complete, each of the Y and N counts in the WRCM would be 12 — half the moduli product.

Now we know what we are looking for. We need 1 elementary rule with an A, 2 with a B, and 5 with a C in row C1 to give us an 8, 8, and 8 count, respectively. In row C2, we need 5 Ys and 3 Ns to give us two 12 counts, and so on. The process of filling in the missing rules is somewhat of a trial-and-error procedure (unless we go to the extreme of a complete classical expansion), but it generally does not take too much time or labor. Sometimes, combining any possible groups of existing rules (disregarding actions) will somewhat speed up the process. None of the initial rules, however, appear to be combinable in this example.

Looking at only rules starting with an A, we note that C2 is short 1 Y. In row C2, rule 1 contains no Ys, the dash in rule 2 represents 2 Ys, and rule 3 represents 1 Y. Row C3 is short 1 N since rule 1 holds 1 N, rule 2 holds none, and rule 3 represents 2 Ns. Similarly, C4 is shy 1 Y. We can now add a rule, rule 8, that will complete the A set.

	1	2	3	8	WRCM A	Y	N
C1	A	A	A	A	8		
C2	N	–	–	Y		4	4
C3	N	Y	N	N		4	4
C4	Y	–	N	Y		4	4
CC	1	4	2	1 = 8			

We now have all 8 of the C1 As.

Next we look at the B set — rules 4 and 5. We need 2 more Bs to bring the count to 8, and we'll try to get both in one (CC=2) rule. Row C2 has 4 Ys (CC=4 in rule 4) and 2 Ns (CC=2 in rule 5). Hence we need a pair of Ns to balance the Ys and Ns.

In row C3, there are 2 Ys and 2 Ns due to the CC=4 dash in rule 4, and in rule 5 there are 2 Ys (CC=2), so again we need a balancing pair of Ns. In row C4, rules 4 and 5 both have dashes, so the Ys and Ns are equal at 3 each, but we need 4 each, so we'll add a dash in our new rule, 9, and the B set is complete:

	3	4	9	WRCM B	Y	N
C1	B	B	B	8		
C2	Y	N	N		4	4
C3	–	Y	N		4	4
C4	–	–	–		4	4
CC	4	2	2 = 8			

Finally, we wish to complete the C set. However, there are only 3 Cs in row C1, so we need 5 more. Since C2, C3, and C4 each have modulus 2, we cannot get 5 rules into one column. Recall that modulus 2 rules can only combine pairwise to yield CCs of 2, 4, 8, 16, 32, 64, etc. Thus, as a minimum, we need at least two C rules, one with a CC=1 and one with a CC=4.

Let's try for the CC=1 rule first by determining which rows have an even number of Ys and an odd number of Ns or vice versa, or, in general, are not in Y and N balance.

In row C2, we have 3 Ns (2 in rule 6 and 1 in rule 7). Thus, we suspect our new CC=1 rule needs an N, and we can pick up all 4 Ys in a separate (CC=4) rule. In row C3, we have 2 Ys in rule 6 and 1 N in rule 7. Hence, a good guess is that our added CC=1 rule needs an N, and we can pick up the other 2 Ys and Ns with a dash in a separate (CC=4) rule. Finally, in row C4 there is 1 N and 1 Y in rule 6, and 1 N in rule 7. Here it looks like we could use another Y to fill in the new CC=1 rule and a dash in the separately added CC=4 rule.

It should now be apparent that we determined both missing C rules in the process of looking for just one of them, and our C set is also completed.

	6	7	10	11	WRCM C	Y	N
C1	C	C	C	C	8		
C2	N	N	N	Y		4	4
C3	Y	N	N	–		4	4
C4	–	N	Y	–		4	4
CC	2	1	1	4 = 8			

If we took the trouble to assemble the new A, B, and C sets into one table, we would find our table is now complete and the missing (and now added) rules were 8, 9, 10, and 11. Furthermore, our WRCM would now be complete:

	A	B	C	Y	N
C1	8	8	8		
C2				12	12
C3				12	12
C4				12	12

7.5. NEGATIVE LOGIC

When an extended condition value is shown *primed* (with an apostrophe or single quote), it means that the particular rule is executed for *all values* except for the one shown. For example, if an extended entry can take on the values 1, 2, 3, or 4 (for a modulus of 4) and a particular entry is 3', this means that the rule is executed for all other values only. That is, the rule is executed for 1, 2, or 4, but *not* for 3.

The decision matrix of a complete, mechanically perfect DT employing negative logic is shown in Fig. 7.7. The complications introduced by negative logic result from the treatment given the

	1	2	3	4	5	6	7	8	9	10	M	Y	N	1	2	3	4	—	WDC	DEL	DOM
C1	Y	Y	Y	Y	Y	Y	N	N	N	N	2	6	4					0	0	2	3
C2	1	1	2	2	3	4	2	2'	3	3'	4			4	4	3	3	0	0	6	
C3	Y	N	Y	N	—	—	Y	Y	N	N	2	4	4					2	4	0	
CC	1	1	1	1	2	2	1	3	1	3=16:16											

Fig. 7.7. A negative logic example.

column counts (CCs), the explicit row count matrix (RCM) entries, and the dash and weighted dash counts (WDCs).

In computing a column count, a primed entry is counted as one less than the modulus of its row. For instance, in Fig. 7.7, rules 8 and 10 each have a CC=3 because 2′ represents 1, 3, and 4 (3 values equally) and 3′ represents 1, 2, and 4 (also 3 values), and all other entry values in these rules are explicit. On the other hand, *primed entries are not dashes,* so they do not contribute to the dash count or to the WDC. Rather, primed entries contribute to the explicit counts in the RCM, with the values not *shown!* Thus, 2′ adds one to each of the explicit 1, 3, and 4 counts, and 3′ adds one to each of the 1, 2, and 4 counts. Therefore, the total of counts in row C2 of the RCM is 4+4+3+3+0=14, which is no longer equal to the total number of rules (10), as we have come to expect.

The table of Fig. 7.7 already has been row sorted by sorting in (top-down) ascending WDCs and subsorting in (top-down) ascending DELs (within the two equal WDCs of C1 and C2). And C2 is above C3, which it dominates by virtue of the 4 in row C2, rule 6, over a dash in C3. An ensuing furcation attempt gives

	1	2	3	4	5	6	7	8	9	10
C1	Y	Y	Y	Y	Y	Y	N	N	N	N
C2	1	1	2	2	3	4	2	2′	3	3′
C3	Y	N	Y	N	–	–	Y	Y	N	N

which reveals a need to further sort the lower-right C2–C3 by the R7–R10 submatrix. By eyeballing, we easily get

	7	8	9	10
C3	Y	Y	N	N
C2	2	2′	3	3′

and the implementing decision tree is shown in Fig. 7.8.

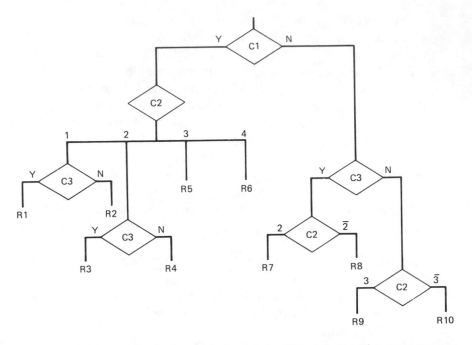

Fig. 7.8. Decision tree for the negative logic example of Fig. 7.7. Note that overscores may be used in place of primes.

7.6. AN EXAMPLE OF DUAL DECOMPOSITION

Another complete and fully sorted decision matrix employing negative logic is pictured in Fig. 7.9. Again observe the effects on CCs in rules 5 and 8 and the "oversize" total in the C4 entries of the RCM.

In Fig. 7.9, C2 and C3 were subsorted in ascending DELs, but the overall row sort did not result in ascending WDCs because C4 had to be placed under the more dominant C3 (the 3 Ns and C3 were used to flag the 3 dashes in C4). Also note that C2, C3, and C4 all have equal dash counts. However, this sorting does furcate smoothly in one pass:

	1	2	3	4	5	6	7	8	9	10	11	12	13
C1	Y	Y	Y	N	N	N	N	N	N	N	N	N	N
C2	–	–	–	1	1	1	2	2	2	3	3	3	3
C3	–	–	–	Y	Y	N	Y	Y	N	Y	Y	Y	N
C4	1	2	3	1	1'	–	2	2'	–	1	2	3	–

	1	2	3	4	5	6	7	8	9	10	11	12	13	M	Y	N	1	2	3	-	WDC	DEL	DOM
C1	Y	Y	Y	N	N	N	N	N	N	N	N	N	N	2	3	~10				0	0	7	2,3
C2	-	-	-	1	1	1	2	2	2	3	3	3	3	3			3	3	4	3	18	2	
C3	-	-	-	Y	Y	N	Y	Y	N	Y	Y	Y	N	2	7	3	3	3	4	3	18	4	4
C4	1	2	3	1	1'	-	2	2'	-	1	2	3	-	3			4	4	4	3	9	4	
CC	6	6	6	1	2	3	1	2	3	1	1	1	1	3 = 36:36									

Fig. 7.9. Another negative logic example.

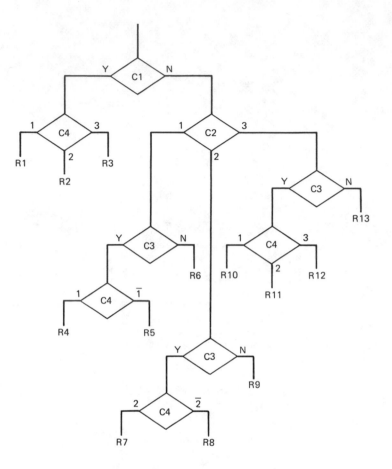

Fig. 7.10. Decision tree for the first furcation.

Its decision tree is drawn in Fig. 7.10.

The invariance of the C2–C3–C4 dash count and the overriding dominance of C3, since they do not lead to any subsorting requirements, tend to arouse one's curiosity as to whether there may be other ways to decompose this problem. Sure enough, some juggling of the Fig. 7.9 matrix does lead to another matrix structure that furcates readily:

	1	2	3	4	5	7	8	10	11	12	6	9	13	–	WDC	DEL
C1	Y	Y	Y	N	N	N	N	N	N	N	N	N	N	0	0	7
C3	–	–	–	Y	Y	Y	Y	Y	Y	Y	N	N	N	3	18	4
C2	–	–	–	1	1	2	2	3	3	3	1	2	3	3	18	2
C4	1	2	3	1	1′	2	2′	1	2	3	–	–	–	3	9	4

Its decision tree is illustrated in Fig. 7.11.

For the first furcation pictured in Fig. 7.10, there are nine decisions requiring that nine tests be stored during execution. Assuming all rules are equally likely to occur, rule 1 requires that 2 tests be executed, rule 2 requires 2, rule 3 needs 2, rule 4 requires 4, and so on, for a total of 13 rules yielding an average of

$$(2+2+2+4+4+3+4+4+3+4+4+4+3) \div 13 = 41/13 = 3.31$$

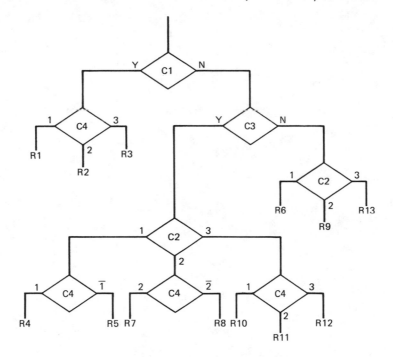

Fig. 7.11. Decision tree for the second furcation.

tests per module execution.

For the second furcation (Fig. 7.11), there are only 8 decision blocks for an improved test storage count of 8 (compared to 9 before), and the individual rule test counts R1, 2; R2, 3; R3, 2; R4, 4; and so on, identical to the last example. Hence, assuming equal probabilities for all 13 rules, we again get an average of 3.31 tests per execution.

Note in the second furcation above that C3 and C2 were subsorted in (top-down) *descending* DELs rather than in ascending order as dictated by the Section 4.3 furcation guide. Thus, our guide does not necessarily lead to the most optimum program and it is now apparent that, in general, a given DT may be sequentially implemented by more than one set of tests.

8
Optimization

8.1. INTRODUCTION

On the evening of January 16, 1970, the author heard Dr. Richard W. Hamming deliver in New York City a lecture titled "One Man's View of Computer Science." This lecture was an updated version of his 1968 Turing Award lecture of the same title (12). The theme of Dr. Hamming's lecture was that individual programmers could not continue to write programs in their own particular undisciplined way with little regard for others who might have to understand them (document, use, debug, or modify them) at some later date. Dr. Hamming said that programmers would have to change their ways and adopt some limited set of standards lest the world become populated with more differently styled programs than could possibly be maintained. And he said that needed new techniques were evolving. He was right, for software engineering had just started.

Since then, the emphasis has been on understandable and orderly programs and systems, not on individualized, tricky, superefficient, anything-goes coding.

This chapter is to be devoted to DT-optimization schemes — they are fun! But as we are aware, optimization has taken a backseat to style, structure, organization, and maintainability. Thus, it will generally not be appropriate or worth our effort to strive for super-efficient or elegant DT implementation (unless, perhaps, we were developing a DT processor, which is not the concern of this text).

Rather, we will most often prefer a less efficient but orderly DT that is relatively easy to develop, understand, implement, and maintain, as we have been doing consistently throughout this book as we decomposed DTs with the aid of our furcation guides. Actually, these are *the* most important factors to optimize.

Attempting to optimize DTs with regard to speed of execution or needed storage space is usually pointless. Other factors, including the features of the operating system used and the data structures chosen, often dominate overwhelmingly.

However, sometimes we can improve the efficiency of a DT with relatively little effort and no loss in clarity. In fact, we may likely improve the clarity of the actions.

8.2. QUICK AND DELAYED RULES

An appropriate starting place for studying DT-optimization rules is Michael Montalbano's work (24, but see also 32 and 33), which introduced two algorithms, a "quick-rule" method to minimize storage of decision tests, and a "delayed-rule" method to minimize average execution time of decision tests. In the *quick rule,* a DT is organized to isolate rules as quickly as possible. In the *delayed rule,* a DT is organized to delay as long as possible the isolation of the rules.

An "incomplete" table is shown in Fig. 8.1. Here, of the $2 \times 2 \times 2 \times 4 = 32$ elementary rules, only 6 can be expected to occur. Thus, the other 26 rules officially cannot happen and we will treat this table as physically complete.

The original version developed from the functional specs is pictured in Fig. 8.1(a). Since there are no dashes in this table, our main row-sorting guides are absent and we have primarily just the DELs to steer us — no dash count, no WDC, and no DOMs. Anyway, the original version furcates readily:

	1	2	3	4	5	6
C1	Y	Y	Y	Y	Y	N
C2	Y	Y	Y	Y	N	N
C3	Y	Y	Y	N	N	N
C4	A	B	C	D	C	B

The extraneous B, C, D, and Ns can be treated as exclusive don't-cares.

	1	2	3	4	5	6	A	B	C	D	Y	N	–	DEL
C1	Y	Y	Y	Y	Y	N					5	1	0	4
C2	Y	Y	Y	Y	N	N					4	2	0	2
C3	Y	Y	Y	N	N	N					3	3	0	0
C4	A	B	C	D	C	D	1	2	2	1			0	2

a. Original version

	1	2	3	4	5	6	A	B	C	D	Y	N	–	DEL
C1	Y	Y	Y	Y	Y	N					5	1	0	4
C2	Y	Y	Y	Y	N	N					4	2	0	2
C4	A	B	C	D	C	D	1	2	2	1			0	2
C3	Y	Y	Y	N	N	N					3	3	0	0

b. Descending DEL's

	1	2	3	4	5	6	A	B	C	D	Y	N	–	DEL
C3	Y	Y	Y	N	N	N					3	3	0	0
C2	Y	Y	Y	Y	N	N					4	2	0	2
C4	A	B	C	D	C	B	1	2	2	1			0	2
C1	Y	Y	Y	Y	Y	N					5	1	0	4

c. Ascending DEL's

Fig. 8.1. An "incomplete" table with different row sorts.

Examining this furcation or its decision tree in Fig. 8.2, we note 4 tests, so our storage count (of test code) is 4. During execution of this DT, rules 1, 2, and 3 take 4 tests each, rule 4 takes 3 tests, rule 5 takes 2 tests, and rule 6 takes 1 test. Therefore, if we assume that all 6 rules occur with equal frequency, then the average number of tests per execution is

$$(3 \times 4 + 3 + 2 + 1) \div 6 = 18/6 = 3$$

The quick rule implies that we sort our table in *descending* DELs, as we did in Fig. 8.1(b). This way, for example, we immediately expose rule 6, then rule 5, and so on, as the furcation illustrates:

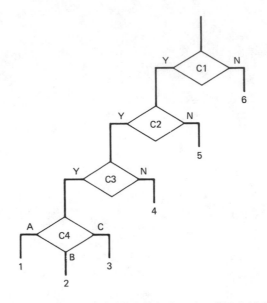

Fig. 8.2. Decision tree for the original version (Fig. 8.1[a]).

	1	2	3	4	5	6
C1	Y	Y	Y	Y	Y	N
C2	Y	Y	Y	Y	N	N
C4	A	B	C	D	C	B
C3	Y	Y	Y	N	N	N

Here again the extraneous B, C, Ys, and Ns are treated as exclusive don't-cares.

A study of the descending DEL furcation and its decision tree in Fig. 8.3 reveals a storage count of 3 (stored decision tests), and, assuming all rules are equally likely, the average number of tests per execution is

$$(4 \times 3 + 2 + 1) \div 6 = 15/6 = 2.5$$

The delayed rule implies a row sort in *ascending* DELs as in Fig. 8.1(c). In this case we keep the tree, at each level of decomposition,

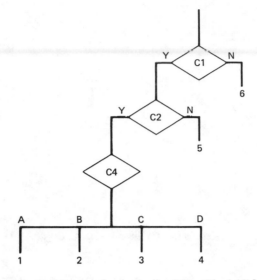

Fig. 8.3. Decision tree for descending DELs (Fig. 8.1[b]).

as balanced as possible to delay isolating a single rule. For example, C3 in Fig. 8.1(c) is perfectly balanced with 3 Ys and 3 Ns, so no rules at all are isolated at the first test. Furcating this case gives

	1	2	3	4	5	6
C3	Y	Y	Y	N	N	N
C2	Y	Y	Y	Y	N	N
C4	A	B	C	D	C	B
C1	Y	Y	Y	Y	Y	N

yielding the tree of Fig. 8.4.

This furcation and the tree in Fig. 8.4 give us a storage count of 4. Next we note that rules 1, 2, 3, and 4 each take 2 tests, and rules 5 and 6 each require 3 tests. Hence, the average number of tests is

$$(4 \times 2 + 2 \times 3) \div 6 = 14/6 = 2.33$$

Summarizing these figures, we get

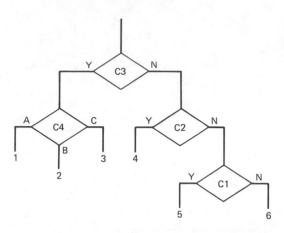

Fig. 8.4. Decision tree for ascending DELs (Fig. 8.1[c]).

	STORAGE	EXECUTION
ORIGINAL DT	4	3
QUICK RULE DT	3	2.5
DELAYED RULE DT	4	2.33

for the number of tests stored and the average number of tests executed. Clearly, for this case, the quick rule tended to decrease decision storage (note STORAGE=3) and the delayed rule tended to decrease decision execution time (note EXECUTION=2.33).

Now we have examples of a complete table, including don't-cares (Figs. 7.9, 7.10, and 7.11), and an "incomplete" table, with explicits only (Figs. 8.1, 8.2, 8.3, and 8.4), which furcate readily in more than one way and lead to different implementation costs (in terms of storage and execution time).

Montalbano also treated don't-cares and rule probabilities (where the more probable rules are exposed more quickly using a modified delayed-rule method). He notes that optimization taking account of the relative frequencies or probabilities is rarely worth the work (24). His statement is true for low-activity situations, but certainly is not true for high-activity situations. Low-activity and high-activity situations are contrasted by the frequency with which one uses a particular DT rule. For example, a person with a checking account typically makes fewer deposits (a low-activity situation) than the number of checks he writes (a high-activity situation). Rules that identify high-activity situations should be isolated first.

We will not treat the remaining of Montalbano's rules or most of the myriad methods, additions, modifications, and so on, that have been generated over the subsequent years. In general, they tend to be too mathematical, too laborious, or of limited value when one considers the manual development of DTs in daily work.

Instead, in the next section we will present a pair of simplified, but quite adequate and practical, sets of decision matrix structuring rules as organized by Frank Dapron (9).

8.3. A PRAGMATIC PAIR OF DECISION MATRIX STRUCTURING RULES

Dapron's preliminary organization of a DT involves what we have already been doing — using simple codes for extended entries and using symbolic designations for rule columns (Rs), condition rows (Cs), action rows (As), and exit rows (Xs). Then he develops the numerics — CCs, Ms, RCMs, WDCs, DELs, and DOMs, as we have been doing throughout most of the text. He also finishes with a re-sort to place dominant rows above the rows they dominate and column sort "on any fixed collating sequence." Thus, with the support of the furcation guide (Section 4.3), which originally stemmed from Dapron's rules, we can condense his decision-matrix rules to simply a few significant statements.

One rule is for general design and documentation purposes. Its significant features are given below:

OPTIMIZING CONDITIONS
FOR
DESIGN AND DOCUMENTATION

1. Sort rows on ascending dash count.
2. Subsort rows on ascending DELs within equal values of dash counts.
3. Determine dominances in a top-to-bottom sequence.
4. Flag don't-cares used in determining dominances by crossing them out.
5. When determining dominances, search upward only to unflagged don't-cares.

The only differences between our furcation guide and the above rule is that in the above rule, no requirement is made for a row free of dashes, the initial sort is on dash counts rather than WDCs, and only on upward dominance searches are we restricted to unflagged dashes.

Dapron's other rule is strictly for sequential testing, as has been our concern so far. Its significant features, assuming no rule-probability considerations, are given as follows:

OPTIMIZING CONDITIONS

FOR

SEQUENTIAL TESTING

1. At least one condition row must contain no dashes (otherwise, it is necessary to expand a minimum dash row to eliminate dashes).
2. Sort rows on ascending WDCs.
3. Subsort rows on ascending DELs within equal values of WDCs.
4. Calculate dominances as in steps 3, 4, and 5 of the prior rule.

As we can see, this is our furcation guide except for our refusal to reuse any dash in a dominance calculation.

A decision matrix that has been sorted according to the design and documentation rule is drawn in Fig. 8.5. As should readily be apparent to us by now, it would need considerable reworking to optimize it for sequential testing. C1 or C2 would have to be expanded to give us a row without dashes. Then, a re-sort into ascending WDCs would be required. New column sorting would be needed. And some sub-

	1	2	3	4	5	6	7	8	9	10	11	12	13	M	–	WDC
C1	Y	Y	Y	Y	N	N	N	N	N	N	N	N	–	2	1	6
C2	Y	Y	N	N	Y	Y	Y	Y	Y	N	N	–	N	2	1	2
C3	–	–	A	A'	A	B	C	C	D	A	B'	B	A'	4	2	8
C4	Y	N	–	Y	–	N	Y	N	–	N	Y	Y	N	2	3	6
CC	4	4	2	3	2	1	1	1	2	1	3	2	6 = 32:32			

Fig. 8.5. A DT optimized for documentation.

matrix sorting would probably be required to make it completely decomposable.

8.4. A SEQUENTIAL PROBABILITY EXAMPLE

A complete DT with known relative rule frequencies or probabilities is shown in Fig. 8.6. The probability (P) of a given rule occurring during any execution of this DT is tabulated directly below its CC (for example, rule 1 occurs about 20% of the time and rule 2, about 10%). Note that the sum of all the probabilities is 100% — as it must be.

Dapron's rule for sequential testing, when rule frequencies are used, requires that we weight the RCM entries by the probabilities and the WDCs by the product of the probabilities and the CCs. Observe that in row C1, the Y probabilities are (rules 1–7)

$$0.2 + 0.1 + 0.1 + 0.1 + 0.1 + 0.15 + 0.15 = 0.90,$$

and the sum of the Y and N probabilities is 1.00. So the respective Y, N, and – entries are 0.9, 0.1, and 0, respectively.

In row C4, the A probabilities sum to (rules 1, 8, and 10) 0.2 + 0.02 + 0.02 = 0.24, the B probabilities to (rules 2, 3, 9, and 11) 0.1 + 0.1 + 0.01 + 0.01 = 0.22, the C probabilities to (rules 4, 5, 9, and 11) 0.1 + 0.1 + 0.01 + 0.01 = 0.22, and the dash probabilities to (rules 6, 7, 12, and 13) 0.15 + 0.15 + 0.01 + 0.01 = 0.32, for a grand total of 1.00. Note that we are assuming rules 9 and 11 each split their 2% probabilities equally between B and C — 1% each.

The DELs, as usual, are the differences of the explicits in the RCM. For example, the difference between Y and N in row C2 is 0.68 – 0.32 = 0.36, and in row C4 the DEL is the absolute value of 0.24 – (0.22 + 0.22) = 0.24 – 0.44 = –0.20, or 0.20 without the sign.

For the WDCs we use the product, P × CC, to determine values. For instance, in row C3 (rules 1–7), these products add like so:

$$0.8 + 0.2 + 0.2 + 0.2 + 0.2 + 0.9 + 0.9 = 3.4$$

Row sorting on WDCs, subsorting on DELs, then column sorting gives us the following furcation:

	1	2	3	4	5	6	7	8	9	10	11	12	13	A	B	C	Y	N	−	WDC	DEL	DOM
C1	Y	Y	Y	Y	Y	Y	Y	N	N	N	N	N	N				.90	.10	0	0	.8	C3,C5
C2	Y	Y	Y	Y	Y	N	N	Y	Y	Y	Y	N	N				.68	.32	0	0	.36	C4
C3	−	−	−	−	−	−	−	Y	N	Y	N	Y	N				.05	.05	.90	3.4	0	
C4	A	B	B	C	C	−	−	A	A'	A	A'	−	−	.24	.22	.22			.32	1.92	.20	
C5	−	Y	N	Y	N	Y	N	−	−	−	−	−	−				.35	.35	.30	1.16	0	
CC	4	2	2	2	2	6	6	2	2	2	4	6	6 = 48									
P	.20	.10	.10	.10	.10	.15	.15	.02	.02	.02	.02	.01	.01 = 1.00									
P×CC	.80	.20	.20	.20	.20	.90	.90	.04	.04	.04	.08	.06	.06									

Fig. 8.6. A DT with known rule probabilities.

	2	3	4	5	1	8	10	9	11	6	7	12	13	WDC	DEL
C2	Y	Y	Y	Y	Y	Y	Y	Y	Y	N	N	N	N	0	0.36
C1	Y	Y	Y	Y	Y	N	N	N	N	Y	Y	N	N	0	0.80
C5	Y	N	Y	N	–	–	–	–	–	Y	N	–	–	1.16	0
C4	B	B	C	C	A	A	A	A'	A'	–	–	–	–	1.92	0.20
C3	–	–	–	–	–	Y	N	Y	N	–	–	Y	N	3.40	0

The lower-left 3-by-5 matrix did not furcate. However, it should be recognized that in this submatrix, A in C4 dominates the rule 1 dash in C5 (which was not flagged in the first sorting pass), so placing C4 above C5, we get

	1	2	3	4	5
C4	A	B	B	C	C
C5	–	Y	N	Y	N
C3	–	–	–	–	–

Our furcation is complete.

The resulting decision tree is drawn in Fig. 8.7. Here we see that the higher probability rules (rule 1, 20%, and rules 6 and 7, 15% each) only require 3 tests, whereas the lower probability rules each went through a sequence of 4 tests before reaching their action sets.

Had we ignored the rule probabilities and used our prior methods, the DT sort and furcation would have been quite different. However, it would have resulted in the implementation given in Fig. 8.8 – which is just as good as that of Fig. 8.7! That is, the higher probability rules (1, 6, and 7), while following different sequences, were reached just as fast. Similar results, in addition to the lack or instability of frequency data, lead to limited attempts to account for rule probabilities in sequential testing, except in high-activity situations. Optimization for space or speed in DTs is rarely worth the work.

8.5. PARALLEL TESTING

In LEDT parallel testing, all of the condition answers in a rule are tested simultaneously (from, for instance, left to right), rather than

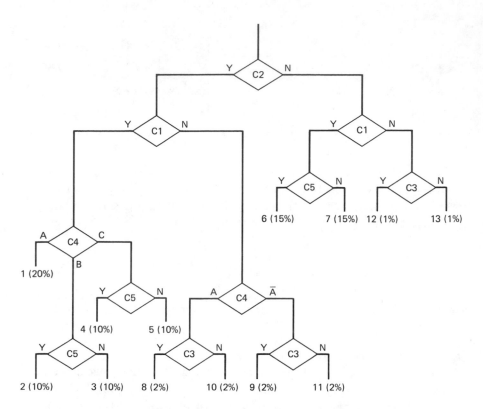

Fig. 8.7. **Decision tree for the table with known rule probabilities.**

testing one condition at a time (normally top to bottom), as in sequential testing. Parallel testing is expensive because it adds a fixed overhead to the condition-testing process. Furthermore, it requires that DTs be sorted in a manner different than that for sequential testing.

The row sort may be of no particular consequence except for presentation or documentation purposes. However, if the thing being tested is, for example, a bit string of flags, then the row sort would probably be such that the top-to-bottom sequence of tests matches the storage sequence of the flag bits.

Similarly, there may be no initial column-sorting requirements. However, if the relative frequencies (but not necessarily the exact probabilities) of pattern occurrences is known, then the column sort would likely be left to right in descending order of relative frequencies.

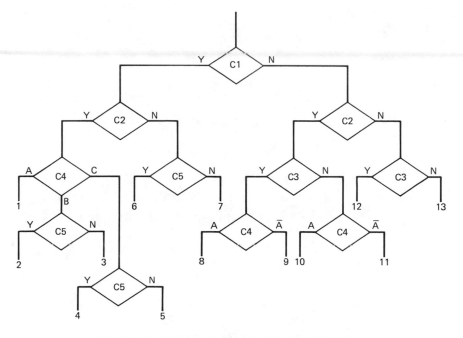

Fig. 8.8. Decision tree developed without probabilities.

A table is shown in Fig. 8.9(a) that tests a 3-bit string of flags stored in C1–C2–C3 sequence. Also, the 5 rules are column sorted left to right from the pattern most likely to occur (rule 1, about 50%) to the pattern least likely to occur (rule 5, about 2%). If the relative frequencies are not known, the column sort could be in any pleasing order.

In DT processors, two matrices that represent this DT can be constructed (see Kirk [16] and King [17]). One is called the *mask* and is formed by replacing all the dashes by 0s and all the explicit Ys and Ns by 1s as in Fig. 8.9(b). The other matrix is called the *test standard* and is formed by replacing all dashes and Ns by 0s and all the Ys by 1s, as was done in Fig. 8.9(c).

During an execution of the DT, the bit string being tested is ANDed (refer to Chapter 10, Boolean Algebra) bit by bit with each of the mask patterns (from left to right) until the resulting bit string, after ANDing, matches the test-standard bit string in the same rule.

To clarify this procedure, suppose in a given automated execution of our DT the current set of flags to be tested is 010, where 0 repre-

	1	2	3	4	5
C1	N	Y	N	N	Y
C2	–	Y	N	Y	N
C3	Y	–	N	N	–
P	.50	.30	.10	.08	.02 = 1.00

a. DT in descending rule probabilities

	1	2	3	4	5
C1	1	1	1	1	1
C2	0	1	1	1	1
C3	1	0	1	1	0

b. Mask

	1	2	3	4	5
C1	0	1	0	0	1
C2	0	1	0	1	0
C3	1	0	0	0	0

c. Test standard

Fig. 8.9. A DT for parallel testing.

sents an N and 1 represents a Y in storage. As we can see from Fig. 8.9(a), this set of flag values calls for the execution of rule 4 (NYN).

In an automated search procedure, the 010 flag bits are ANDed with the 101 pattern of rule 1 in Fig. 8.9(b), giving us a 000 result that does *not* match the rule 1 001 pattern in the test standard of Fig. 8.9(c).

Next, 010 is ANDed with the 110 pattern of rule 2 in Fig. 8.9(b) to give 010, which does *not* match the rule 2 110 pattern in Fig. 8.9(c). Then, 010 is ANDed with 111 (rule 3, Fig. 8.9[b]) to give 010, which does *not* match the rule 3 000 (Fig. 8.9[c]).

Finally, the flags 010 are ANDed with the rule 4 mask bits 111 (Fig. 8.9[b]) to yield 010, which *does* match the test-standard rule-4 pattern of 010. Hence, we have systematically, in a left-to-right order, uncovered the proper rule to be executed.

By placing our rules in descending order of probability, the more likely rules require the fewest bit-pattern tests, giving us an execution-time optimization. In our example, rule 1 occurs 50% of the time and only requires one test (and one comparison). For instance, if the flag bits were 001 (or 011), then upon being ANDed with the rule-1 mask pattern of 101 we would get 001, which immediately matches the rule-1 standard of 001.

Rule 2 requires 2 tests and comparisons, rule 3 needs 3 tests, rule 4 needs 4, and rule 5, which only occurs 2% of the time, requires the maximum of 5 ANDings and comparisons to isolate the proper action set.

8.6. OPTIMIZING ACTIONS

When designing a DT by longhand, the author has found that the furcation rule of Chapter 4 is generally a quite satisfactory guide for organizing the *condition* structure of the table. However, we have said very little yet about organizing the actions, except that they should be in top-to-bottom execution sequence.

Some practitioners number their action selections instead of simply using a selection X, and some DT processors also will permit this scheme. Several benefits can accrue from such a practice. First, it explicitly shows the required sequence of actions. Second, if the order of some actions does not really matter, they can be given the same number. For example, for rule 1 in the DT of Fig. 8.10,

	1	2	3	4	5
C1	Y	Y	N	N	N
C2	–	–	Y	N	N
C3	Y	N	–	Y	N
A1	1			1	1
A2		1	2	1	3
A3	2	2	1	1	2
A4	2	3			
X1	3		3	2	
X2		4			4

Fig. 8.10. A DT with numbered action selections.

	1	2	3	4	5	6	7	8	9	10	11
C1	Y	Y	Y	Y	Y	Y	Y	N	N	N	N
C2	Y	Y	N	N	N	N	N	Y	Y	N	N
C3	–	–	A	A	B	C	C	–	–	–	–
C4	–	–	–	–	–	Y	N	–	–	Y	N
C5	Y	N	Y	N	–	–	–	–	–	–	–
C6	–	–	–	–	–	–	–	Y	N	–	–
A1		X					X				
A2		X					X				
A3	X					X					
A4								X	X		
A5								X			
A6								X	X		
A7				X							X
A8		X					X				
A9	X		X		X	X				X	
A10								X	X		
X1				X							X
X2		X					X				
X3	X							X	X	X	

Fig. 8.11. A DT with X action selections.

since the order in which A3 and A4 are executed does not matter, they are both given the selection number 2, which, in turn, gives the designer (or processor) more freedom in optimizing action groupings. Third, if one rule requires certain actions in one sequence and another rule requires the same actions in another sequence, both rules can be accommodated without listing an action more than one time. In Fig. 8.10, rule 2 executes A2 before A3, but rules 3 and 5 each execute A3 before A2, and rule 4 does not care which execution order is employed.

An example of an X table is outlined schematically in Fig. 8.11. This is a complete table, fully condition sorted, and we wish to see what can be done to improve the action clarity and efficiency of this module (Dapron [9]).

	4	11	2	7	1	6	5	3	10	8	9	C
A1			X	X								1
A2			X	X								1
A3					X	X						1
A4										X	X	2
A5										X		1
A6										X	X	1
A7	X	X										1
A8			X	X								1
A9					X	X	X	X	X			2
A10										X	X	1
												12
X1	X	X										
X2			X	X								
X3					X	X	X					
X4								X	X	X	X	

Fig. 8.12. Actions column sorted.

Isolating the actions only, we first column sort to get common action sequences together. This is done in Fig. 8.12 for our example, using the exit grouping as our main initial guide. Note here that if the A4–A5 sequence did not matter (as might be revealed by numbered selections), we could place A5 ahead of A4, permitting us to get by with but one copy of A4. That is, underlined groupings indicate that only one copy of the action coding need be stored. But as things stand, rules 8 and 9 cannot use the same copy of A4 because only rule 8 must execute A5 next. The C column at the right tabulates the *copy counts* for the various actions, and we observe that only actions A4 and A9 must be coded twice (because their two copies are followed by different actions or exits) in the implementation of this DT.

Next, we row sort in order to get closer visual groupings of common action sequences together, without violating the top-to-bottom sequences in any particular rule. This has been done in Fig. 8.13.

Then we see if we can apply a couple of common procedures to reduce the copy counts. Our objective is not necessarily to reduce

	4	11	2	7	1	6	5	3	10	8	9	C
A4										X	X	2
A5										X		1
A6										X	X	1
A10										X	X	1
A3					X	X						1
A9					X	X	X	X	X			2
A1			X	X								1
A2			X	X								1
A8			X	X								1
A7	X	X										1
												12
X1	X	X										
X2			X	X								
X3					X	X	X					
X4								X	X	X	X	

Fig. 8.13. Actions row sorted.

the total copy count, but rather to reduce any individual copy counts where the individual actions represent more than a few lines of coding.

For example, if A4 is a CALL to (DO of) a large subroutine or an INCLUDE of a large block of code, then it may be worth our while to reduce its copy count from 2 to 1. If we examine our original DT in Fig. 8.11, we note that the only difference between the condition patterns in rules 8 and 9 is the answer to C6.

Now, if, and only if, action A4 does not have any effect on test C6, then A4 can be hoisted into the condition half of our table directly above C6. In this event, only one copy of A4 would be needed since there is only one path of events ahead of it. For sake of illustration, we will assume A4 is a large block of code that does not influence C6.

Let us also assume that A9 represents a large amount of processing. The trick here is to place a switch setting ahead of A9, in rules 1, 6, and 5, to turn on the switch (presumed off at module entrance) and then interrogate it after A9, thus separating the two exits (X3 for rules 1, 6, and 6, and X4 for rules 3 and 10).

	4	11	2	7	1	6	5	3	10	8	9	C
A4										X	X	1
C6												
A5										X		1
A6										X	X	1
A10										X	X	1
A3					X	X						1
A11					X	X	X					1
A9					X	X	X	X	X			1
C7					Y	Y	Y	N	N			
A1			X	X								1
A2			X	X								1
A8			X	X								1
A7	X	X										1
												11
X1	X	X										
X2			X	X								
X3					X	X	X					
X4								X	X	X	X	

Fig. 8.14. Action hoisted with switch added to reduce copy counts.

In Fig. 8.14, A4 has been hoisted above C6 to reduce its copy count to 1. Also, an added action A11 (turning on the "do exit 3 rather than exit 4 switch") has been placed about A9 and then tested with an added condition C7 after A9 to cause a reduction in the A9 copy count. And, as is obvious, we are starting to permit actions in the upper condition quadrants and conditions in the lower action quadrants – a practice that adds complications and hence is taken only with much caution.

The final step is to place the DT back into its original condition-oriented column sort (Fig. 8.11), but retain all our action-row sorting (Fig. 8.14) and not lose our copy-count improvements. These things have been done in Fig. 8.15. The copy-count reduction is clear from the right parentheses on the right of all but one X in each action row. The right parenthesis indicates a branch to the single true copy on the left that has no right parenthesis.

	1	2	3	4	5	6	7	8	9	10	11
C1	Y	Y	Y	Y	Y	Y	Y	N	N	N	N
C2	Y	Y	N	N	N	N	N	Y	Y	N	N
C3	–	–	A	A	B	C	C	–	–	–	–
A4								X	X)		
C4	–	–	–	–	–	Y	N	–	–	Y	N
C5	Y	N	Y	N	–	–	–	–	–	–	–
C6	–	–	–	–	–	–	–	Y	N	–	–
A5								X			
A6								X	X)		
A10								X	X)		
A3	X					X)					
A11	X				X)	X)					
A9	X		X)		X)	X)				X)	
C7	Y	–	N	–	Y	Y	–	–	–	N	–
A1		X						X)			
A2		X						X)			
A8		X						X)			
A7				X							X)
X1				X							X)
X2		X						X)			
X3	X				X)	X)					
X4				X					X)	X)	X)

Fig. 8.15. Final DT with action optimizations.

9
Procedural Copying to
Produce A DT

9.1. COPYING A FLOWCHART

A given flowchart may be copied onto a DT worksheet for purposes of exploiting DT features — insurance of mechanical perfection, optimizing conditions or actions, standardization, compactness of presentation, input to a DT compiler, and so on. However, as we started to do in the last chapter (Section 8.6 on actions), we will have to loosen up our original "pure" four-quadrant scheme where only conditions appear in the upper quadrants and only actions in the lower quadrants.

In fact, we may place actions in the condition stub as soon as we recognize that sufficient tests have been made to warrant the actions. In particular, we may wish to start the condition stub with a set of module-initialization actions. If this initialization set is very large, we may wish to limit our DT start to a single action, CALL (table name), where the invoked DT may sometimes be an *action-only table* (contains no condition stub at all). Putting actions in the condition stub other than at the start can be dangerous if the actions may alter any condition.

Our SHOOT A GAME table (Fig. 6.15) could have been made more complete and functional if it had included the action of rolling the dice as its very first entry in the condition stub. Then the invoking modules would not have had to prepare for the invocation by rolling the dice first. In general, it appears to be good software engineering to have all modules initialize themselves with a leading block of code so that the modules are more complete and more likely to be reusable.

Similarly, there is no reason (at least in manual DT design) why we cannot have conditions or conditional actions as well as CALL (table name) actions (which could, in turn, be any kind of DT, including action-only types) in the action quadrants. Such mixing of conditions and actions do not, in general, invalidate our optimization or furcation techniques, providing we are careful to preserve any necessary vertical sequencing. And, of course, the calculation of our numerics is totally unaffected.

A small and more or less typical flowchart is sketched in Fig. 9.1. To convert it to DT format, we may proceed in an orderly manner, as from left to right, tracing every possible path from the entry to the exit, giving these paths rule numbers as we trace. In Fig. 9.1, we uncover 5 paths leading to the 5 rules in the DT of Fig. 9.2.

Note that in Fig. 9.2 we placed the CCs at the bottom of the table so that we would not forget to include C4, which was imbedded in the action stub. Also note that initial condition-stub actions, such as A1, must be X'd all across the row since *all* rules include these actions.

This DT turned out to be mechanically perfect. Had it not been so, our DT would have quickly revealed defects – particularly if we next compared the resulting DT with the functional specs. In any

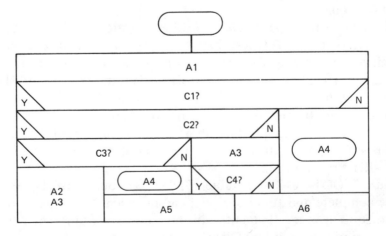

Fig. 9.1. A Chapin chart with mixed actions and decisions.

	1	2	3	4	5
A1	X	X	X	X	X
C1	Y	Y	Y	Y	N
C2	Y	Y	N	N	–
C3	Y	N	–	–	–
A2	X				X
A3	X		X	X	
A4		X			X
C4	–	–	Y	N	–
A5		X	X		
A6				X	X
X1	X	X	X		
X2				X	X
CC	2	2	2	2	8 = 16

Fig. 9.2. DT for the mixed flowchart.

event, we now have our module in DT form and can therefore employ any desired DT manipulation schemes.

9.2. COPYING A HIPO DIAGRAM

A typical detailed HIPO diagram (15) is drawn in Fig. 9.3. In such a diagram, the left major black is labelled INPUT and contains all pertinent data items (records, transactions, parameters, and so on) fed into the module and its subordinates. The center PROCESS block contains in execution sequence the activities performed by the module and its subordinates. The OUTPUT block illustrates all outputs from the module and its subordinates (messages, records, codes, parameters, and so on). The INPUT-PROCESS-OUTPUT is the IPO part of HIPO – Hierarchical Input-Process-Output. The H part of HIPO is a hierarchical structure diagram, called a "visual table of contents" or VTOC.

To prepare a flowchart or DT from a HIPO diagram for a module or segment, we simply follow the sequence of activities in the PROCESS block from top to bottom. That we have done in Fig. 9.4 in DT

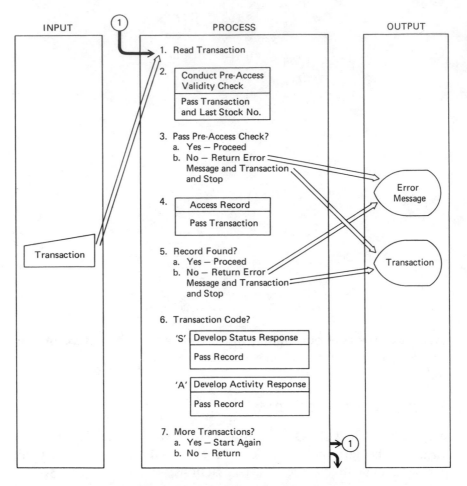

Fig. 9.3. An example of a detailed HIPO diagram.

format. The correlation between Figs. 9.3 and 9.4 should be obvious.
In this instance, we happen to get again a mechanically perfect table.

We should also begin to realize that when actions and conditions
are mixed, it becomes somewhat arbitrary where we draw the lines
between the condition and action stubs — though all the permanent
exits must always be lower than the lowest condition. For example,
in Fig. 9.4 we could have drawn the lines below C3 and let C4 be a
condition in the action stub. At least by placing the lines below C4,
though, our action and exit stubs were "pure."

HIPO TABLE		1	2	3	4	5	6	M
A1	READ TRANSACTION	X	X	X	X	X	X	
A2	CALL PRE-ACCESS VALIDITY TABLE	X	X	X	X	X	X	
C1	PASS PRE-ACCESS CHECK	Y	Y	Y	Y	Y	N	2
A3	CALL ACCESS TABLE	X	X	X	X	X		
C2	RECORD FOUND	Y	Y	Y	Y	N	–	2
C3	TRANSACTION CODE	A	A	S	S	–	–	2
A4	CALL ACTIVITY TABLE	X	X					
A5	CALL STATUS TABLE			X	X			
C4	MORE TRANSACTIONS	Y	N	Y	N	–	–	2
	CC	1	1	1	1	4	8 = 16:16	
A6	TRANSMIT ERROR MESSAGE					X	X	
A7	TRANSMIT TRANSACTION					X	X	
X1	GO AGAIN	X		X				
X2	RETURN		X		X	X	X	

Fig. 9.4. DT for the HIPO diagram.

9.3. STRUCTURED PROGRAMMING

The requirements of structured programming (28) have been observed tacitly throughout this book since structured programming is an important part of software engineering. The three basic control patterns of structured programming are diagramed in ANSI flowchart and Chapin-chart form in Fig. 9.5.

Three extensions of these basic patterns are also acceptable and useful, and diagramed in Fig. 9.6. One is the "case" or n-way branch. Note that it too, like the binary or 2-way branch, requires a confluence or fan-in (rejoining) of the lines of control flow. The second pattern is the following-decision loop or following-decision iteration. As in FORTRAN, this one executes first and then asks about the exit, instead of testing the exit condition first. The third pattern is the general pattern of which the leading-decision (do-while) and following-decision (do-until) are special cases. This general iteration pattern is the loop-exit-if. Here, as in Fig. 9.5, an initialization and a termination for the iteration are included in Fig. 9.6.

Sequence

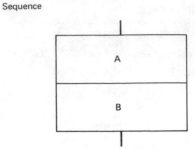
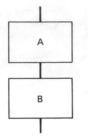

Selection

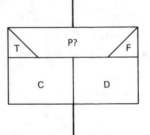
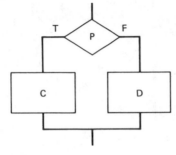

Iteration

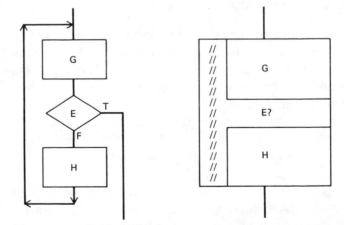

Fig. 9.5. The three basic control patterns of structured programming.

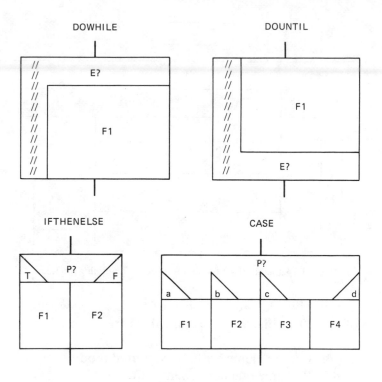

Fig. 9.6. Four extended control patterns for structured programming.

9.4. COPYING A STRUCTURED MODULE

The Chapin chart for a structured programming module is pictured in Fig. 9.7. Note that its overall structure consists of a set of nested IF-ELSEs — the outer P1, a separate P2 nested on each side of the P1, and a P3 nested on the false side of the rightmost P2.

The inner structure contains several sequences, such as the F1–F2, which, in turn, is in sequence with F3 along the left side. Another is the sequence of F2–F3 along the right edge. Also, there is a DOUNTIL of F4 against P5 and a three-way CASE of F3, F2, and F7 against P4, which is in sequence with F8. Finally, we see a sequence of F1 with a DOWHILE of F5–F6 against P6.

In the Chapin chart of Fig. 9.7, we can trace every path threading through this structured programming module from its single entry to

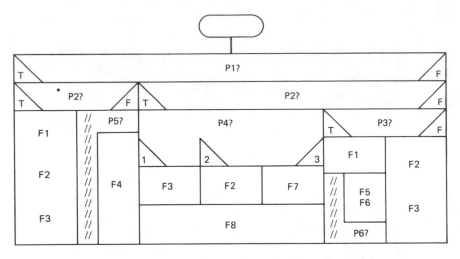

Fig. 9.7. A Chapin chart for a structured programming module.

its single exit. By a left-to-right scan of these paths, we obtained the 7 rules of the DT in Fig. 9.8. Several things are of note here:

1. Since we are dealing with a structured module, all rules must end in the same one permanent exit.
2. The normal structure of limited entries in a DT naturally accommodates IF-ELSEs and nested IF-ELSEs.
3. By codifying an extended entry to successive positive integers starting with 1, a normal DT naturally accommodates a CASE.
4. By making actions conditional, a DT can be made to accommodate iterations easily. For example, we used UNTIL P for a DOUNTIL and WHILE P for a DOWHILE. Alternatively, we could have easily extended the condition stub, thereby increasing the number of decision rules.

In summary, not only is it fairly simple to fit a structured program module into a DT, but knowing how to make such fits guides us in developing DTs that yield structured modules and programs in the first place. The rules are simple:

1. Permit only one permanent exit per module (DT).
2. Codify extended condition entries with successive positive

		1	2	3	4	5	6	7	M
C1	P1	Y	Y	N	N	N	N	N	2
C2	P2	Y	N	Y	Y	Y	N	N	2
C3	P3	–	–	–	–	–	Y	N	2
C4	P4	–	–	1	2	3	–	–	3
	CC	6	6	2	2	2	3	3 = 24:24
A1	F1	X					X		
A2	F2	X		X				X	
A3	F3			X				X	
A4	F4 UNTIL P5		X						
A5	F5 WHILE P6						X		
A6	F6						X		
A7	F7	X				X			
A8	F8			X	X	X			
X1	RETURN	X	X	X	X	X	X	X	

Fig. 9.8. DT for the structured programming module.

integers starting with 1.
3. Provide explicitly for iteration.

9.5. WHICH WAY TO GO

The process of copying from a Chapin chart, HIPO, and the like, has some value in doing quality assurance work. But the more common need is to go in the other direction — to produce a Chapin chart or HIPO from a DT. This is often demanded "for documentation purposes." To help meet this need, the earlier chapters in this book have stressed the equivalent representation for DTs in Chapin charts, with some use of decision trees, semicode, and flow diagrams. If well prepared, all of these tools should show a good correspondence with each other.

10
Boolean Algebra

10.1. BRIEF REVIEW

No attempt shall be made herein to teach the work of George Boole, the more practical engineering forms of Boolean algebra (13), or the modern mathematical set-theory approach. However, a very brief refresher should be helpful for those who do not make frequent or involved use of these concepts. Also, it will help us to establish a particular notation for our use. A detailed knowledge of Boolean algebra, though, is *not* necessary for successful programming applications of DTs. Hence, the reader may skip to Chapter 11 at any point.

Boolean algebra deals symbolically and graphically with variables that can assume only two states (or values), which can be designated True and False or Yes and No or On and Off or High and Low or Good and Bad, and so on. In the modern engineering forms, and when automated, these two values are generally represented by the binary digits 0 and 1, where most often the 1 is the more positive or affirmative value – True, Yes, On, High, Good.

The most popular set of Boolean operations is the NOT, OR, and AND set. The NOT is illustrated in Fig. 10.1. It is sometimes called *complementation* or *logical negation*. It simply implies that if we are given one value for a variable, its NOT is the complement, or other value. Thus,

$$\text{NOT}\,(0) = 1$$
$$\text{and NOT}\,(1) = 0$$

A	NOT
0	1
1	0

Fig. 10.1. A truth table of the NOT operation.

The OR and AND operations can involve any number of variables. They are shown in a tabular form, called a truth table, for three independent variables, in Fig. 10.2.   The independent-variable columns can be filled in by imagining a binary counter (of 3 bits in this example), filling it with all zeros, and then advancing the count by 1 at a time (as we fill in the rows top down) until the counter is completely filled to capacity — all ones. (Note that the rows are generally numbered according to the apparent binary counter value.) In general, then, there are 2^N rows, where N is the number of independent variables. In our $N = 3$ example, we get $2^3 = 8$ rows.

The OR (also known as the *inclusive* OR) represents a "mixing" action and is also known as *union* or *logical sum*. Here, if we are given several variable values, the OR of these values gives us a 1 if, and only if, *one or more* of the independent variables has a 1 value. For some three-variable examples,

$$OR\ (0,0,0) = 0$$
$$OR\ (0,0,1) = 1$$
$$and\ OR\ (1,0,1) = 1$$

as should be clear from row numbers 0, 1, and 5, respectively, of the OR table in Fig. 10.2.

The AND represents a "coincidence" condition and is also known as *intersection* or *logical product*. If we are given several variable values, the AND is a 1 if, and only if, *all* of the independent variables have a 1 value. For some three-variable examples,

$$AND\ (0,0,0) = 0$$
$$AND\ (0,1,1) = 0$$
$$and\ AND\ (1,1,1) = 1$$

Row No.	A	B	C	OR	AND	NOR	NAND
0	0	0	0	0	0	1	1
1	0	0	1	1	0	0	1
2	0	1	0	1	0	0	1
3	0	1	1	1	0	0	1
4	1	0	0	1	0	0	1
5	1	0	1	1	0	0	1
6	1	1	0	1	0	0	1
7	1	1	1	1	1	0	0

Fig. 10.2. Three-variable truth tables for the basic OR, AND, NOR, and NAND connectives.

as should be apparent from row numbers 0, 3, and 7, respectively, in Fig. 10.2.

The NOR is simply the complement of the OR (*NOT* of the *OR*), and the NAND is simply the complement of the AND (*NOT* of the *AND*). For example, in row number 1 (second row),

$$OR\ (0,0,1) = 1$$
$$giving\ NOR\ (0,0,1) = 0$$
$$and\ AND\ (0,0,1) = 0$$
$$giving\ NAND\ (0,0,1) = 1$$

Also, we frequently have need for a *two*-variable *exclusive* OR (EO) in both problem exposition and in computer languages. The two-variable exclusive OR *excludes* the coincidence of both independent variables having a 1 value, as shown in Fig. 10.3. For example, while

$$OR\ (1,0)\ =\ EO\ (1,0) = 1\ in\ row\ number\ 2$$
$$the\ OR\ (1,1)\ =\ 1$$
$$but\ EO\ (1,1)\ =\ 0\ in\ row\ number\ 3$$

Some of the symbols employed are tabulated below for various computer languages, mathematics, and engineering:

	NOT	OR	AND	NOR	NAND	EO
Programming						
Languages						
APL	~	∨	∧	⩡	⩟	≠
ASSEMBLY						
(S/370)		O	N			X
GPSS		+	*			
PL/1	¬	|	&			
COBOL	NOT	OR	AND			
Mathematics						
	~	∨	∧			
(prime)	'	∪	∩			
(overscore)	−		*			
Engineering						
(prime)	'	+	X			⊕
(overscore)	−		· (dot)			

In APL, there really is no EO; However, the ≠ primitive comparison dyadic function gives the proper results when operating on two Boolean values or variables. PL/1 has its own special NOT symbol, ¬, and uses the vertical bar, | , for the OR. Most often, outside of programming languages, the NOT is represented by a following prime (apostrophe or single quote), an overscore, or a preceding tilde, ~. In engineering, AND is represented by an ordinary product − X, ·, *, or simply the *juxtaposition* of two symbolic variables (separated and each placed in parentheses if necessary); for example, AXB, A·B, AB, A*B, or (A) (B).

Row No.	A	B	OR	EO
0	0	0	0	0
1	0	1	1	1
2	1	0	1	1
3	1	1	1	0

Fig. 10.3. Two-variable truth tables for the *inclusive* OR and the *exclusive* OR.

Row No.	A	B	C	F
0	0	0	0	0
1	0	0	1	0
2	0	1	0	0
3	0	1	1	1
4	1	0	0	0
5	1	0	1	1
6	1	1	0	0
7	1	1	1	1

Fig. 10.4. A particular function of three variables.

For a simple example of a Boolean function, let the independent variable A represent the presence of Alice, B the presence of Betty, and C the presence of Carol in the playroom. That is, A=1 if Alice is in the playroom and A=0 if she is not. And the function (dependent variable) we are to develop, F, represents a potential two-handed card game of gin rummy.

The functional specs for our potential game of gin are:

1. Alice will only play with Carol.
2. Betty will only play with Carol, but not if there is an audience.
3. Carol will play with anyone.

Our function, F, is tabulated in Fig. 10.4, where rows 0, 1, 2, and 4 clearly permit no gin games (because gin requires *two* players). Row 6 is also discounted since Alice and Betty will not play together. Row 3 has Betty and Carol playing, and row 5, Alice and Carol. Row 7 also has Alice and Carol playing because Alice will not play with Betty who will not play with Carol while Alice, an "audience," is there.

Covering the function's 1's in a common engineering form, we get

$$F(A,B,C) = A'BC + AB'C + ABC$$

For example, if row 3 applied,

$$F(0,1,1) = 0' \times 1 \times 1 + 0 \times 1' \times 1 + 0 \times 1 \times 1$$
$$= 1 \times 1 \times 1 + 0 \times 0 \times 1 + 0 \times 1 \times 1$$
$$= 1 + 0 + 0$$
$$= 1$$

and we *do* have a game — Betty and Carol. And if row 6 applied, we would have

$$F(1,1,0) = 1' \times 1 \times 0 + 1 \times 1' \times 0 + 1 \times 1 \times 0$$
$$= 0 \times 1 \times 0 + 1 \times 0 \times 0 + 1 \times 1 \times 0$$
$$= 0 + 0 + 0$$
$$= 0$$

and we do *not* have a game — Alice and Betty will not play with each other.

In PL/1 our dependent function, F, would be

$$\neg A\&B\&C \mid A\& \neg B\&C \mid A\&B\&C$$

but in APL it would be

$$((\sim A) \wedge B \wedge C) \vee (A \wedge (\sim B) \wedge C) \vee A \wedge B \wedge C$$

because APL uses a right-to-left (function-of-a-function) scan of operators (APL functions) rather than a priority scheme, requiring separating or overriding parentheses progressively as we move to the left.

In the given engineering form and in PL/1, NOT has the highest priority (all NOTs are executed first), AND has the next lower priority (all ANDs are executed second), and OR has the lowest priority (all ORs are executed last), except when overridden by parenthetical groupings.

If we are skilled in the identities of Boolean algebra (13), we could freely manipulate our function into a variety of forms in our quest for some kind of optimum. For our function,

$$F = A'BC + AB'C + ABC$$

the distributive law would permit "factoring" out the logical AND with C to give

$$F = (A'B + AB' + AB)C$$

One of the elementary propositions would allow us to repeat the AB term for

$$F = (A'B + AB' + AB + AB)C$$

Then, commutation would permit

$$F = (AB + AB' + AB + A'B)C$$

Next, the distributive law gives

$$F = [A(B + B') + (A + A')B]C$$

and another elementary proposition allows

$$F = (A \times 1 + 1 \times B)C$$

Yet another elementary proposition yields

$$F = (A + B)C$$

which reads "there will be a gin rummy game if either Alice OR Betty (or both — inclusive OR) AND Carol are in the playroom."

The truth table 1s of Fig. 10.4 have been transferred to the much more efficient map (13) of Fig. 10.5. Here, one familiar with map methods immediately recognizes the two "compatible pairs" of 1s and writes

$$F = AC + BC = (A + B)C$$

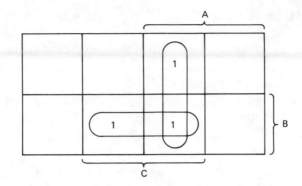

Fig. 10.5. Modified Karnaugh map of the given three-variable problem.

10.2. DT CONVERSION

Any DT can be converted to LEDT form. For example, if we have
the modulus 4 extended entry (from Fig. 2.12):

	1	2	3	4
COLOR	R	G	B	Y

we can change this to the mutually exclusive diagonal of limited
entries (from Fig. 2.11):

	1	2	3	4
RED	Y	N	N	N
GREEN	–	Y	N	N
BLUE	–	–	Y	N

In turn, any mechanically perfect LEDT without an ELSE rule can
be converted into a truth table set of Boolean functions. The technique is to convert all Ns, explicit or from dashes, to 0s and all Ys,
explicit or not, to 1s, and then reorient the table to conventional
truth-table form.

The ORDER TABLE (Fig. 3.1) in symbolic form (Fig. 4.2) is redrawn in Fig. 10.6. If we treat conditions C1, C2, and C3 as independent variables, place them along the top of the table, then classically expand all rules to get rid of dashes, we would have a truth table presentation as in Fig. 10.7.

Note that we pick up a potentially desirable degree of freedom in going from the DT to the truth-table format. In a truth table, a "rule" need not have a column count which is a power of two. Rather, we deal now in functions rather than rules, and all rules that lead to the same action-exit set are normally consolidated into one function regardless of column counts.

Comparing the DT to the truth table, we observe that R1 in Fig. 10.6 is Y for all three conditions, corresponding to three 1s in row 7 in the truth table of Fig. 10.7. Next, R2 is YYN, which is 110 in the truth table. Finally, both R3 (C1 = Y and C2 = N) and R4 (C1 = N) lead to the same action set. Hence, R1 maps into F1, R2 into F2, and R3 *and* R4 into F3.

As we learned earlier, writing out classical expansions is prohibitive for more than a handful of independent variables (conditions). However, in practice, one skilled in Boolean algebra would skip the truth table and go directly to the much more efficient form of a truth map. This we have done in Fig. 10.8 for our ORDER TABLE. An extra bonus picked up here is that for a mechanically perfect DT,

	R1	R2	R3	R4
C1	Y	Y	Y	N
C2	Y	Y	N	–
C3	Y	N	–	–
A1	X			
A2	X			
A3		X		
X1	X			
X2			X	X
X3		X		

Fig. 10.6. ORDER TABLE from Chapters 3 and 4.

we get a truth map whose every 2^N inner square is exactly filled once, and once only, with a function symbol.

If any inner square (logical AND – intersection of condition values) is empty, we have a missing elementary rule; if any inner square is filled with two or more of the same function symbols, we have a re-

Row No.	C1	C2	C3	F1	F2	F3
0	0	0	0	0	0	1
1	0	0	1	0	0	1
2	0	1	0	0	0	1
3	0	1	1	0	0	1
4	1	0	0	0	0	1
5	1	0	1	0	0	1
6	1	1	0	0	1	0
7	1	1	1	1	0	0
A1				X		
A2				X		
A3					X	
X1				X		
X2						X
X3					X	

Fig. 10.7. Truth tables for ORDER TABLE functions.

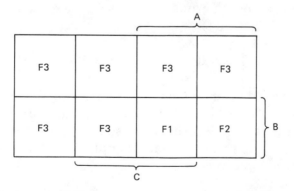

Fig. 10.8. Modified Karnaugh map for ORDER TABLE functions.

dundancy; and if any inner square is filled with two or more different function symbols, we have a serious pathology — contradictions.

10.3. IMPLEMENTATION

The map of Fig. 10.8 can be read in any of the permissible Boolean algebra forms, of which there are basically eight (13, Chapter 4), but actually an unlimited number can be derived from the free use of Boolean identities. We will only sample a very few to give us a feel for the design freedom offered. Also, we will no longer use a flowchart or Chapin chart to represent our implementation.

Until now, Chapin charts and flowcharts have served us well as relatively simple yet disciplined ways to illustrate the implementation of our furcated DTs. However, we will not be furcating DTs in this chapter, but instead abstracting and algebraically manipulating Boolean functions. While Boolean logic can be read from Chapin charts, it requires going deeper into Boolean logic than this chapter goes.

For example, one of the basic forms of an EO (exclusive OR) of two variables, the AND/OR (13, p. 104), is

$$EO(A,B) = AB' + A'B$$

which can be readily identified in a decision tree as shown in Fig. 10.9.

In a flowchart or Chapin chart, a sequence of decisions can form an AND, and several paths brought together can form an OR. Thus, a flowchart can nicely fit an AND/OR Boolean form. However, an exclusive OR (or any other function) can also be manipulated to the OR/AND form (13, p. 104):

$$EO(A,B) = (A + B) (A' + B')$$

This form would require a flowchart in which the true of A is tied to the true of B, which is then placed in sequence with the false of A tied to the false of B. The words sound reasonable, but it cannot be done on a flowchart in a meaningful, direct fashion. And we have hardly begun to explore all the alternative Boolean forms of any given function.

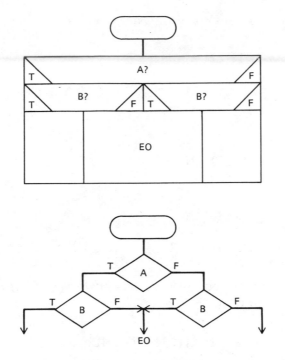

Fig. 10.9. Exclusive OR traced in a decision tree.

Thus, we will use a computer language for illustrating Boolean implementations of conditions. From our chart in Section 10.1, it looks like PL/1 or APL would be good selections since they each contain our main three tools – NOT, OR, and AND. However, PL/1 will probably be clearer to most readers.

From the truth table of Fig. 10.7 or the truth map of Fig. 10.8, F1 and F2 are most simply

$$F1 = C1 \& C2 \& C3$$

$$\text{and } F2 = C1 \& C2 \& \neg C3$$

F3 is clearly all decision paths where either C1 or C2 is negative. Thus,

$$F3 = \neg C1 \mid \neg C2$$

Our module content could thus be coded as

```
IF C1&C2&C3 THEN
   DO;
      A1;
      A2;
      X1;
   END;
IF C1&C2&¬ C3 THEN
   DO;
      A3;
      X3;
   END;
IF ¬ C1 | ¬ C2 THEN X2;
```

However, another Boolean identity, known as *De Morgan's theorem*, would permit our third IF to be coded as

$$IF ¬ (C1\&C2) \text{ THEN } X2$$

Moreover, coupling our knowledge of PL/1 with Boolean algebra and a mechanically perfect situation, we might now recognize that we could have coded the module as follows:

```
IF C1&C2 THEN
   IF C3 THEN
      DO;
         A1;
         A2;
         X1;
      END;
   ELSE
      DO;
         A3;
         X3;
      END;
ELSE X2;
```

In this implementation,

$$F1 = (C1 \& C2) \& C3$$

$$F2 = (C1 \& C2) \& \neg C3$$

$$\text{and } F3 = \neg (C1 \& C2)$$

we used the $(C1 \& C2)$ term only once in the first line of coding, though it serviced all decisions.

Here we note that nested IFs are like ANDing, ELSEs are like NOTing, and our last rule must be everything else because we have a mechanically perfect module.

10.4. CONCLUSION

It is the author's experience and conviction that DTs are a big improvement over traditional flowcharts as a design tool. Moreover, it should now be apparent that DTs do not exclude the use of many popular techniques, such as HIPOs, Chapin charts, semicode, PDL, and so forth. In addition, the application of Boolean algebra appears to offer an advantage over the use of DTs alone for computer languages with flexible condition operations and efficient compiling.

However, as in the case of the more complex and detailed refinements to DT processing, the use of Boolean algebra could also be an uneconomic refinement. That is, with the possible exception of DT processor designs for certain specific languages, the practical, everyday use of our earlier, relatively simple furcation methods may be in our best interest instead.

Boolean algebra was introduced primarily for two reasons. First, it does form the foundation for DTs themselves and much of the analytical work in the literature. And second, if the reader *is* quite proficient in Boolean algebra and map techniques, this chapter may aid in the development of some programs or modules (for certain languages) that do reward the extra effort.

11
Processors

11.1. CLASSIFICATION

Decision-table *processors* are software programs that automate some or all of the steps leading to the ultimate execution of DTs. They appear to divide into three general categories (27):

1. *Interpreters.*
2. *Compilers* [also known as *automatic converters* (32)].
3. *Translators* [also known as *semiautomatic converters* (32)].

For *interpretive* conversion, the DTs themselves (generally in a compact coded form — as suggested, in part, by the mask and test-standard matrices of parallel testing in Section 8.5) are placed in storage during execution. Then the interpreter, through a set of its subprograms, executes the input program directly, accepting the DTs as data. This type of processor tends to run rather slowly (32) and is not too common. However, it offers the advantage of having easier program maintenance than the other types of processors because debugging and modification are always made directly to the DTs, and documentation is therefore always up to date.

In *compiler* conversion, the DT is written in a source language. The source language is generally a high-level language, either a general-purpose type (COBOL, FORTRAN, PL/1, APL) or a special-purpose subject-matter-specialist type (such as GPSS or SIMSCRIPT for simulation work) with special DT compiler statements. The compiler completely converts the DTs to machine object code. Decision-table compilers potentially yield fast and efficient programs, but they are inflexible from the standpoint of being machine dependent (32).

By far, the most common form of DT processor is the *translator* type of converter. Here the output of the processor is a source language — most often a general-purpose, high-level language. Thus, the output must be compiled or assembled, altogether a two-step procedure. However, modern efficient conversion techniques can be used in developing the DT processor, and it does not tend to be machine dependent.

The DTs for translators are generally written in a combination of special processor *key words* (verbs) and statements, plus statements that are identical to (or very close to) those of the output source-language itself. Thus, if a translator outputs COBOL, its DT condition and action stubs look much like COBOL statements; if it outputs PL/1, most of its DT condition and action statements may be for-matted almost as if lines of PL/1 code were being written, and the same can be done with other source languages.

The reader should be cautioned here that, frequently, any one of the terms — *compiler, translator,* or *preprocessor* — is used loosely, or even interchangeably, to indicate *any* type of DT-automated con-version. The term *preprocessor* is common because many DT trans-lators are *pre*processors to some common high-level language, such as COBOL or PL/1. That is, the COBOL or PL/1 compiler accepts DTs as preprocessor input statements. Also, many of us tend to think of all language converters as translators or compilers, so the general use of *these* terms is also quite understandable.

11.2. LANGUAGES

In the past, many well-known DT processors have been COBOL and FORTRAN translators. The large number of COBOL translators is due to two factors (besides the general popularity of COBOL for nonmathematical work). First, business-applications programmers tend to be table-oriented (and, hence, are more likely to favor the use of DTs than, say, a systems programmer). Second, much of the early well-publicized processor work utilized COBOL.

In September 1962, the CODASYL Systems Group presented a symposium paper titled "Preliminary Specifications for a Decision Table Structured Language – DETAB-X." The language used was COBOL and certain amenable revisions to COBOL resulted. Later, the specifications for the COBOL translator, DETAB-65, was prepared by Working Group 2 on Decision Tables of the SIGPLAN of the Los Angeles chapter of the ACM. Then DETAB-66 was developed by Anson Chapman of North American Aviation, and, later, DETAB-67 by the Dow Chemical Company (for interal use only).

There are obvious reasons for having many FORTRAN translators. FORTRAN has been popular for mathematical and engineering applications. Also, a noticeable part of mathematical and engineering applications has been logic-oriented (for example, in the qualification of probabilistic statements in set theory, and, in particular, the layout of computer logic circuits). And, as we know, DTs represent a tabular form of logic.

To a lesser extent, translators have also been developed that produce source code in other languages, such as ALGOL, AUTOCODER, and ASSEMBLY. Also, APL is being used as a conversational interpretive terminal language through which a variety of languages can be translated – ALGOL, COBOL, PL/1, an "abstract" DT language, and APL itself.

Especially notable is the more recent emergence of PL/1 translators since PL/1 attempts to include both the business capabilities of COBOL and the mathematical capabilities of FORTRAN.

Information concerning the total number of different DT processors and their languages, however, is difficult to obtain. Many processors are developed for in-house use only in various corporations, schools, and governmental agencies, and many of these have local security classifications and therefore are not known to the public or described in the literature.

11.3. FEATURES

In this section we are concerned with the multitude of characteristics, requirements, limitations, and so forth, that must be considered when one attempts to select a particular DT processor or to decide whether a processor should be used at all. We will simply number the various features of concern without seriously attempting to label or sort them into some kind of priority sequence. In fact, rather than chance omitting some important point, our numbered items may even overlap. (For additional aid, consult Metzner and Barnes [24], McDaniel [28], and Pooch [32].)

We have already considered the types of processors. For ease of discussion, we will assume that the following pertains to the dominant translator type. However, most of the points covered are applicable for all three types.

1. What language does it produce? Are we familiar with this language? Is it appropriate to our applications? Is it maintained? Is it modern, efficient, transferable to other systems?

2. What is the date of its release? A translator written in 1965 is not as likely to have incorporated many of the newer optimization schemes, to have profited from experience with older translators, or to have as long a future as one written in 1985. Almost all translators were first written in the late 1960s. One that dates from the late 1970s is IBM's DTABL.

3. What is its cost? Prices range from free to tens of thousands of dollars. Of course, for the higher priced translators, installation and maintenance are more likely to be available.

4. What are its storage requirements and speed? Here we may be concerned with both the translation process itself and the efficiency of the produced program.

5. Does it produce reliable code? Has it been demonstrated that the code it produces is relatively free of bugs? And can these bugs, if any, be readily detected and corrected (regardless of who does the job) — serviceability?

6. What is the interface for correcting and modifying the produced code? Can changes be made at the desirable DT level, preserving the DT approach in the first place and keeping our documentation current? Or must we work with the produced source code, perhaps with tracing, or worse, must we dig into the dumps of the final machine code?

7. Does the translator produce a wealth of detailed, meaningful error messages to help insure that we have not made

syntax errors, that we do not have missing, redundant, or conflicting rules, and so on?

8. Does a copy of each DT appear in the source-language listing, perhaps with each DT preceding the source code it produced?

9. What is the physical form of entering a DT? Is, for example, each line of a DT entered via a convenient or an inconvenient medium or piece of equipment?

10. Does the translator deal only with single DTs or does it accommodate an entire program? If only single, unrelated, and isolated modules are produced, one per DT, then they must be laboriously link-edited together to form a complete program. A translator, however, may process a whole program or at least feed the individual modules into a common library from which they can be knitted together quite readily. For example, one APL-nested translator (DTABL) produces only individual DTs, but with a choice of several source languages, including PL/1, whereas an extension of this interactive terminal process (DTIPT), using only the PL/1 option of the single DT translator, produces a complete program library of modules.

11. Does it accept vertical or horizontal tables? We have dealt only with vertical tables in this book — that is, we have used a worksheet form in which rules are tabulated vertically. However, that means that each row, when entered into a processor, is most often a single condition, a single action, or a single exit, but includes answers to, or selections from, all the rules. The vast majority of DTs are vertical. A few people, though, prefer to make each entry a complete rule, and some translators (for example, TABSOL) demand a horizontal input. The advantage here is that a single rule can be modified with but one input statement (perhaps a punch card) rather than reentering an entire DT.

12. Does the translator permit, or perhaps demand, a mixture of DTs and source code? A preprocessor that allows mixing of DTs and source code offers more flexibility — and more opportunities for bugs — than does a pure DT interface.

13. Does the translator permit action-only (unconditional) tables? If action-only tables are not accommodated, then

we may not be able to keep the tables desirably small, yet functional.

14. Does it permit an initialization block of coding at the beginning of the table?

15. Does it allow for the insertion of comments that will appear on a listing?

16. Does it encourage the discipline of software engineering?

17. Does it accommodate intermodule parameters?

18. Does it have a rich set of verbs and mechanics that permit flexibility and simplicity in specifying action-only, initialization, comments, parameters, options (for example, MAIN and RECURSIVE in PL/1), and so on?

19. Does it provide for, or even demand, an *ELSE rule?* Some compilers (for example, PET and DETRAN) must be given a mechanically complete DT, or error messages result. Many allow an ELSE as an option (for example, DECIBLE III, DETAB-66, FORTAB, and TABTRAN). At the other extreme, some demand an ELSE rule (DETAB-65).

21. Does it permit extended entries? Many processors only accommodate LEDTs. However, some programmers find such a limitation to be no serious handicap.

22. Does it allow coded action sequencing? Some processors only permit the usual X selection for top-down sequencing, while others provide for quite elaborate and flexible action sequencing codes.

23. Does it sort conditions? Some row and column sort (some using modern and sophisticated optimization techniques, others only relatively simple furcation methods). Some only column sort (for example, PET requires a pre-row-sorted table with no dashes in the top row).

24. Does it sort actions? Most processors at least sort actions to the extent that repeated sequences are tied together and lead to only a single storage for the set. Some, however, do very sophisticated action sorting and may hoist actions into the condition quadrants to cut down on copy counts. Here the user must be very careful that such hoisting will not cause an action to precede a condition that it may alter. If it does, then this processor "option" must be disabled (as in DTABL)

if possible. Else, the processor cannot be used or the DTs must be redesigned to avoid this problem.

25. Does the processor accommodate rule probabilities in its optimization schemes?

26. Does the processor provide for relational operators in the condition stub? For example, SMP uses E for "equal," N for "not equal," H for "greater than," I for "not greater than," L for "less than," and M for "not less than." Some others use EQ (equal), NEQ (not equal), and so on.

27. Is iteration within the DT accommodated? That is, can we loop easily within a DT?

28. How many conditions, actions, and rules are permitted? Some translators separately place a limit, like 50, on each of these three items. Some place a combined limit of about 100 on conditions plus actions. Some place no limit beyond machine storage space. Some place a limit on the number of source statements produced. If ordinary-sized DT worksheets are used and modules are kept desirably small, none of these limits would likely be of concern.

29. How is the horizontal double line inserted in a vertical table? In other words, how do you specify the end of conditions and the beginning of actions? For example, in PET, all conditions and actions are numbered by the user with ascending three-digit decimal numbers. When the first decreasing number is encountered, PET interprets this as the beginning of the actions.

30. How large can the stub entries be? A limit is likely placed on how many characters can be on one line in a condition or action stub However, some processors permit an entry to be continued from one line to another, probably to some maximum number of lines.

Obviously, we have not listed everything that could be thought of or that may be pertinent in a given case. However, the preceding list should be quite adequate for alerting the potential user to the many kinds of considerations involved.

11.4. CONCLUSION

The use of decision tables, in conjunction with modern function parsing techniques from software engineering, represents a superior methodology for solving complex problems and for attaining reliable and well-structured modules, programs, and systems. These benefits may be obtained by converting DTs to code, only using relatively simple furcation rules. However, with the emergence of new flexible processors employing sophisticated optimization schemes, using modern languages, offering full library facilities, and, perhaps, available in on-line conversational form, DT use should be seriously considered in support of the techniques of software engineering.

Bibliography

1. Cantrell, H. N.; King, J.; and King, F. E. H. "Logic structure tables," *Communications of the ACM*, Volume *4*, Number 6 (June 1961), pp. 272-275.
2. Chapin, Ned. "An introduction to decision tables," *DPMA Quarterly*, Volume *3*, Number 3 (April 1967), pp. 2-23.
3. Chapin, Ned. "Function parsing in structured design," *Structured Analysis and Design*, Volume *2* (Maidenhead, UK: Infotech International Ltd., 1978), pp. 25-42.
4. Chapin, Ned. "New format for flowcharts," *Software Practice and Experience*, Volume *4*, Number 4 (October - December 1974), pp. 341-357.
5. Chapin, Ned. "Parsing of decision tables," *Comm. ACM*, Volume *10*, Number 8 (August 1967), pp. 507-510.
6. Chapin, Ned. "Semi-code in design and maintenance," *Computers and People*, Volume *27*, Number 6 (June 1978), pp. 2-12.
7. Chapin, Ned. "Structured analysis and structured design: an overview," *System Analysis and Design in the 1980s* (New York: North Holland, 1981), pp. 199-212.
8. Cheng, Cheng-Wen and Rabin, Jonas. "Synthesis of decision rules," *Communications of the ACM*, Volume *19*, Number 7 (July 1976), pp. 404-406.
9. Dapron, F. E. "The pragmatic use of decision tables in programming system design," *Proceedings of the SDD Programming Symposium, IBM TROO. 1934.* (San Jose, CA: IBM Corp., 1969), pp. 127-146.
10. *Decision Tables* (CSA Standard Z243. 1-1970) Canadian Standards Association. US source: American National Standards Institute, New York.
11. Grad, Burton. "Tabular form in decision logic," *Datamation*, Volume *7*, Number 7 (July 1961), pp. 22-26.
12. Hamming, Richard W. "One man's view of computer science," *Journal of the ACM*, Volume *16*, Number 1 (January 1969), pp. 3-12.
13. Hurley, Richard B. *Transistor Logic Circuits.* (New York: John Wiley and Sons, Inc., 1961), 363 pp.
14. IBM Corp. *Decision Tables, Form GF20-8102.* (White Plains, NY.: IBM Corp., 1962), 28 pp.
15. IBM Corp. *HIPO—A Design Aid and Documentation Technique.* (White Plains, NY: IBM Corp., 1974), 130 pp.
16. Kavanagh, R. F. "TABSOL—a fundamental concept for systems-oriented language," *Eastern Joint Computer Conference*, Volume *18*, (Arlington, VA: AFIPS, December 1960), pp. 13-15,117-136.

17. King, P. J. H. "Conversion of decision tables to computer programs by rule mask techniques," *Communication of the ACM,* Volume *9,* Number 11 (November 1966), pp. 796–801.

18. Kirk, H. W. "Use of decision tables in computer programming," *Communications of the ACM,* Volume *8,* Number 1 (January 1965), pp. 41–44.

19. Langenwalter, D. F. "Decision tables: an effective programming tool," *Proceedings of the 1st SIGMINI Symposium.* (New York: ACM, 1978), pp. 77–85.

20. Lew, A. "Optimal conversion of extended-entry decision tables with general cost criteria," *Communications of the ACM,* Volume *21,* Number 5 (May 1978), pp. 269–279.

21. Lew, A., Tamanaha, D. "Decision table programming and reliability," *Proceedings of the 2nd International Conference on Software Engineering.* (Long Beach, CA: IEEE, 1976), pp. 345–349.

22. London, Keith R. *Decision Tables.* (New York: D. Van Nostrand Co., Inc. 1972), 205 pp.

23. Maes, R. "On the representation of program structures by decision tables: a critical assessment," *The Computer Journal,* Volume *21,* Number 4 (November 1978), pp. 290–295.

24. Metzner, John R., and Barnes, Bruce H. *Decision Table Languages and Systems.* (New York: Academic Press, 1977), 172 pp.

25. Montalbano, Michael. *Decision Tables.* (Palo Alto, CA: Science Research Associates, 1974), 191 pp.

26. McDaniel, Herman. *An Introduction to Decision Logic Tables.* (New York: John Wiley and Sons Inc., 1968), 96 pp.

27. McDaniel, Herman. *An Introduction to Decision Logic Tables.* (New York: D. Van Nostrand Co., Inc., 1978), 124 pp.

28. McDaniel, Herman. *Decision Table Software.* (New York: D. Van Nostrand Co., Inc., 1970), 84 pp.

29. McGowan, Clement L., and Kelly, John R. *Top-Down Structured Programming Techniques.* (New York: D. Van Nostrand Co., Inc., 1975), 318 pp.

30. Nickerson, R. C., "An engineering application of logic-structure tables," *Communications of the ACM,* Volume *4,* Number 11 (November 1961), pp. 516–520.

31. Pollack, Solomon L.; Hicks, Harry T.; and Harrison, William J., *Decision Tables: Theory and Practice.* (New York: John Wiley and Sons, Inc., 1971), 179 pp.

32. Pooch, Udo W., "Translation of decision tables," *Computing Surveys,* Volume *6,* Number 2, (June 1974), pp. 125–151.

33. Reinwald, L. T., and Soland, R. M. "Conversion of limited-entry decision tables to optimal computer programs I: minimum average processing time," *Journal of the ACM,* Volume *13* Number 3 (July 1966), pp. 339–358.

34. Reinwald, L. T. and Soland, R. M. "Conversion of limited-entry decision tables to optimal computer programs II: minimum storage requirement," *Journal of the ACM,* Volume *14,* Number 4 (October 1967), pp. 742–755.

35. Sethi, I. K., and Chatterjee, B. "Conversion of decision tables to efficient sequential testing procedures," *Communications of the ACM,* Volume *23,* Number 5 (May, 1980), pp. 279–285.

Index

Index

Action
   column sort, 121
   defined, 6-7
   entry, 6-7, 9
   hoisted, 123
   numbered, 119-120
   optimization, 119-124
   row sort, 121-122
   sequential, 77
   sort, 120-122
   stub, 6-7
Activity, 110, 113-115
Added rules, 94-97
ALGOL, 150
Alternatives, 2
An action row, 10
AND, 134-137
APL, 1, 5, 137, 139, 148, 150, 152
Assembly language, 1, 5, 137, 150
Asterisk, 2, 68, 92-93, 137
AUTOCODER, 150
Average number of tests (*See also* Optimization), 45, 57-58, 71, 81, 103-104, 106-110

Bifurcation, 39
Binary tree (*See also* Decision tree), 12, 38
Boolean algebra, 134-147

CALL, 16-18
Can't happen, 20
Case, 129, 131-133
CC, 25, 36
Chapin chart, 23, 39, 44, 60, 69-70, 73, 75, 79-80, 83-84, 126, 129-133, 144-145

Check, 10-16
Check-off procedure, 39
Classical expansion, 37, 95, 142
Classical technique, 37, 95, 142
Clean-cut table, 54, 87
Closed table, 17
C*n* condition row, 10
COBOL, 1, 5, 137, 148-150
Column
   count, 25-29
   numbers, 7
   sort, 40-42
Combination of tests, 58
Combining rules, 32-36
Combining technique, 37-39
Completeness, 10-16, 28-29, 36-39
Compound tests, 58
Condition
   definition, 2, 6-7
   dominant, 22
   entry, 6-7
   fell swooper, 22, 25-26
   impossible, 19-20
   in actions, 124-127
   matrix (*See* Decision matrix)
   mutually exclusive, 20
   optimization, 105-119
   recognition, 77
   stub, 6-7
Contradiction, 11
Conversion, 141-144
Copy counts, 121-122

Dash
   count, 29-30, 87, 99

definition, 19, 31, 53–54, 99
 flagged, 31, 53, 68, 81, 85, 111–112
DC, 29–30
De Morgan's theorem, 146
DECIBLE, 153
Decision (*See* Condition)
 matrix, 37–38, 57, 68, 87, 97–98, 100,
  102, 111
 tree, 12, 14, 28, 90–91, 93, 100, 102,
  104, 108–110, 116–117, 145
Decision table
 checking, 10–16
 clean-cut, 54, 87
 closed, 17
 completeness, 10–16, 36–39
 conversion, 141–144
 expansion, 25–28, 37, 48–49
 header, 6–7
 history, 2–4
 incomplete, 90
 missing rules, 93–97
 open, 17
 parts, 6–7
 pathologies, 9, 22
 processor, 5, 148–155
 sorting, 40–42, 87, 92
 use, 4–5
DEL, 29–30, 40
Delayed rule, 106, 108–111
Design, 4, 23, 29, 111
DETAB series, 150, 153
Delta, 29–30, 40
DETRAN, 153
DO, 16
Do loop, 129–133
Documentation, 4, 29, 111–112, 133
Dollar sign, 20, 68, 92–93
DOM, 29, 31, 53–54
Dominance, 31, 53–54, 68, 73, 85, 87, 111
Dominant condition, 22
Don't care, 18–22, 68, 92
Double lines, 6–7
Double rules, 6–7
DT (*See* Decision table)
DTABL, 151–153

EEDT, 12–14, 33
Elementary rules, 11, 14, 16, 20, 25
Elimination of rules, 11

ELSE rule, 93, 153
EO, 136–137
Error rule, 93
Event-driven action, 85
Exclusive don't care, 20, 26, 68, 106
Exclusive OR, 81
Exit, 9, 16–18, 27
 entry, 9
 permanent, 16
 temporary, 16
Expansion, classical, 37, 95
Expansion of rules, 25–28, 37, 48–49
Explicit values, 27
Extended entry decision table, 12–14

Fell swooper, 22, 25–26, 35, 52, 58, 73
Figure of merit (*See also* Optimization), 43,
  45, 57–58
First pass, 24, 47–48, 87
Flagged dash, 31, 53, 68, 81, 85, 111–112
Flow diagram, 39, 43, 59, 129–131
FORTAB, 153
FORTRAN, 1, 5, 129, 148
Frequency, 110, 113–115
Function parsing, 4, 65, 70, 154
Furcation, 32–45, 93

GO AGAIN, 16–18
GO TO, 16
GPSS, 137, 148

Header, 6–7
HIPO, 23, 127–129

I, 19, 68
Inclusive don't care, 19
Incomplete table, 90, 106
Instructions, 2
Interrupt, 17
Iteration, 129–133

Karnaugh map, modified, 141, 143
Keywords, 18, 149

Languages, programming *(See also specific*
  type), 1, 148–153
LEDT, 8, 11–12, 19, 32–34, 153
Level, 48
Limited entry decision table, 8
Logical operations, 134–137

M, 24
Map, 141, 143
Mask matrix, 117–119
Mechanical perfection, 4, 20, 24–29, 40,
    48–52, 142–143, 147
MEDT, 14–16, 35–36
Minimization (*See also* Optimization), 81
Missing rules, 9
Mixed actions and conditions, 126–127
Mixed entry decision table, 14–16
Module
    characteristics, 1, 8, 155
    defined, 1, 4
    development, 4, 46, 65–66
Moduli, 12, 14, 24–29
De Morgan's theorem, 146
Mutually exclusive conditions, 20

N, 9
NAND, 136–137
Negation, 134
Negative fell swooper, 26
Negative logic, 97–104
No, 9
No-dash row, 40, 52
NOR, 136–137
NOT, 134–137
Number of rules, 11–16
Number of tests, 43, 45
Numerics, 29–31
N-way branch, 129, 131

Open table, 17
Optimization, 105–124
OR, 134–137
Overbar, 97–100

Parallel testing, 115–119
Parsing of decision tables, 39, 87, 93
Parsing of functions, 4, 65, 70, 154
Pathology, 9, 22, 68
Perfection, mechanical, 4, 20, 24–29, 40,
    48–52, 142–143, 147
PERFORM, 16
Permanent exit, 16, 27
PET, 153–154
PL/1, 1, 5, 137, 139, 148–150, 152–153
Positive fell swooper, 26
Preprocessor, 149

Prime, 97–100, 137–138
Product of moduli, 14, 25–29
Processors, 5, 148–155
Program and modules, 8

Quadrant, 6–7, 125
Quick rule, 106–108, 110–111

RCM, 29–30, 40, 99
Real-time, 17
Redundant actions, 9
Redundant conditions, 22
Reserved words, 18
RETURN, 16–18
R*n* rule number, 10
Row-count matrix, 29–30, 40, 99
Row numbers, 7
Row sort, 40–41, 52, 80–81, 107
Rule
    added, 94–97
    combining, 32–36
    definition, 6–7, 81
    discovery, 93–97
    elimination, 11
    ELSE, 93
    error, 93
    expansion, 25–26
    probabilities, 110, 113–119
    unique, 27–29

Salient values, 27
Select case, 129, 131–133
Semicode, 23, 39, 44–45, 60–61
Sequential testing, 112–115
SIMSCRIPT, 148
SMP, 154
Software engineering *(See also specific
    topics)*, 1–4, 17–18, 65, 70, 127–133,
    154–155
Sort
    action rows, 121–122
    decision table, 31, 40–42
    definition, 40–42, 87, 92
STOP, 16
Structured programming, 129–133
Stub, 6–7, 9

Table, decision (*See* Decision table)
TABSOL, 152
TABTRAN, 153

Temporary exit, 16
Text
   cases, 4
   number of, 45, 57
   parallel, 115–119
   sequential, 112–115
   standard, 117–119
Top-down approach, 1, 65–66, 76–77
Translator, 5, 148–155
Tree (*See also* Decision tree), 12, 14, 28,
   90–91
Trifurcation, 39
Truth table, 135–138, 142

Unique rule, 27–29, 37–39, 49–52

WDC, 29–30, 40, 87
Weighted dash count, 29–30, 40, 87
Weighted rule count matrix, 94–97
WRCM, 94–97

X, 9
X*n* exit row, 10

Y, 9
Yes, 9